"Rarely do we pause and consider *how* we ought to read. With laser focus on this question Thomas Millay makes the paradoxically compelling case that reflection on this question ought to move us away from reflection toward action, specifically the works of neighbor love. How one reads matters, then, since the very transformation of our hearts, minds, and wills is at stake."

—Mark A. Tietjen
Author of *Kierkegaard, Communication, and Virtue:*
Authorship as Edification

"In recent decades, research has shown that literary reading is in a slow but certain decline in Western society—a trend that has been hastened by the arrival of the smartphone. Why bother to read, one might assume, when there is now an abundance of other engaging options, from Facebook to Netflix? One of the best things about Millay's book is that it speaks to this concern, arguing, in particular, that Søren Kierkegaard's thought offers a nuanced apology for the task of reading. Intriguingly, it turns out, Kierkegaard believes that reading, as a quiet and reflective activity, is essential training for the individual to learn how to *act* well in the world. Thus, Millay's book does a great service: it gives us timely wisdom from a thinker whose understanding of modernity is looking increasingly prescient."

—Christopher B. Barnett
Villanova University

"Reading is on its way back and there is a growing literature relating to what it means to read well. Thomas J. Millay's new book shows that Kierkegaard can make an important contribution to the discussion, as well as reminding us that reading is not an end in itself but is to help us change our lives."

—George Pattison
University of Glasgow

"Thomas Millay's volume performs an astonishing feat: it both edifies the general reader and stretches the Kierkegaard specialist. Its main contention could not be more culturally relevant. In this era of the intensified reading of tweets and posts, it reminds us that the ultimate purpose of reading should not be escapism or the accumulation of data, but rather the transformation of the self, which is nothing less than growth in love for God and neighbor."

—Lee C. Barrett
Lancaster Theological Seminary

"Reading well was once regarded as the first step one takes in a process that leads to the contemplation of God. Augustine and Kierkegaard knew that, each in his own way. Thomas J. Millay judiciously and clearly points us back to them while letting us see the limits of their visions. We can only benefit by reading this elegant book."

—Kevin Hart
University of Virginia

YOU MUST CHANGE YOUR LIFE

You Must Change Your Life

Søren Kierkegaard's Philosophy of Reading

THOMAS J. MILLAY

CASCADE *Books* • Eugene, Oregon

Cascade Books
An Imprint of Wipf and Stock Publishers
199 W. 8th Ave., Suite 3
Eugene, OR 97401

www.wipfandstock.com

PAPERBACK ISBN: 978-1-5326-5662-0
HARDCOVER ISBN: 978-1-5326-5663-7
EBOOK ISBN: 978-1-5326-5664-4

Cataloguing-in-Publication data:

Names: Millay, Thomas J., author.
Title: You must change your life : Søren Kierkegaard's philosophy of reading / Thomas J. Millay.
Description: Eugene, OR: Cascade Books, 2020. | Includes bibliographical
references and index.
Identifiers: ISBN 978-1-5326-5662-0 (paperback) | ISBN 978-1-5326-5663-7
(hardcover) | ISBN 978-1-5326-5664-4 (ebook)
Subjects: LCSH: Kierkegaard, Søren, 1813–1855. | Books and reading—Re-
ligious aspects—Christianity.
Classification: B4378.C5 .M50 2020 (print) | B4378.C5 (ebook)

Manufactured in the U.S.A.   JULY 10, 2020

To Laura Elizabeth Ziemer: "happiness is a radiance that transfigures everyone who is touched by it."

Margaret Penny: the sweet life you carry with you walks with me everywhere, every day.

Miss Lena Dehority: I have always thought that I am more like you than anyone else on this earth. Thank you for making me who I am.

Kristy Millay: your joy continues to sustain. You are with me wherever I go.

Contents

.

Preface

THIS BOOK SERVES TWO fundamental purposes.

First, I hope to give those who are at a point in their lives where they are about to embark on a period of more intensive reading some idea of why such an activity might be valuable. If it is the summer after your senior year of high school and you are about to begin college, this book is for you—though it can also serve those who are just entering graduate school or those who have been reading intensively for a long time but have forgotten why they are doing so.

I aim to achieve this first goal by developing a philosophy of reading: that is to say, an account of what reading is for, and how we should do it. Surprisingly, given that this activity is what many academics spend most of their lives doing, there have been fairly few books published on this subject. Those that are published tend to be theological in nature. For example, I have found Alan Jacobs's *A Theology of Reading* and Paul J. Griffiths's *Religious Reading* to be helpful resources. But most books published on the subject of reading are either: (a) arguments for why you should read a particular canon of texts (Karen Swallow Prior's recent book *On Reading Well* falls into this category), or (b) methods of interpretation, which give you different ways to read a text.[1] But neither of these

---

1. For a general orientation, see for example Eagleton, *Literary Theory*. Recently, there has also been helpful work in the history of reading. See Price,

more popular topics address the deeper question at stake: why should we even read at all? It is this question that a philosophy of reading tries to answer.

Second, this book—if successful—will provide the first extended and comprehensive treatment of Kierkegaard's philosophy of reading. Thus far, this has been a neglected topic in Kierkegaard studies.[2] Much has been written on Kierkegaard's rich and sophisticated theory of communication,[3] but such a topic has to do with how and why one writes and speaks, not how and why one reads. With this in mind, I hope what follows goes some way towards filling in this gap in scholarship.

These two objectives have two different audiences. For the general reader, I hope to provide a useful philosophy of reading that adds depth of purpose to this practice. For the Kierkegaard specialist, I hope to provide a thorough treatment of a neglected topic and in this way advance our highly peculiar discipline.

The book unfolds as follows. The first chapter introduces the rest of the book by succinctly answering three questions: Who was

---

What We Talk about When We Talk about Books; Fischer, *A History of Reading*; and Manguel, *A History of Reading*.

2. The most substantial scholarly treatment I have found is the final chapter of Pattison's *Kierkegaard, Religion and the Nineteenth-Century*, chapter 11, "Learning to read the signs of the times," 222–44. (My thanks to Paul Martens for pointing me to this reference.) Pattison's analysis of Kierkegaard's vision of the good reader in this chapter is primarily formal. He confirms that what Kierkegaard says explicitly about what it means to be a good reader is matched by how he implicitly encourages (through pseudonyms and a variety of rhetorical strategies) his texts to be read. What I provide here thus supplements Pattison by attending to the passages in Kierkegaard where reading is explicitly discussed. It might seem at first that Poole's "Towards a Theory of Responsible Reading: How to Read and Why" in *KSYB* 2002 is a further exception to the rule stated above, but closer inspection reveals that this is not the case. The essay has many virtues, but its topic is Poole's own theory of responsible reading or interpretation, not Kierkegaard's. Aumann's *Art and Selfhood* makes observations similar to the ones I make in what follows, only in relation to the appreciation of art rather than reading. See esp. chapter 6, "The Nature of Art Appreciation," 131–60.

3. See for example Turnbull, "Communication/Indirect Communication"; Tietjen, *Kierkegaard, Communication, and Virtue*; Holmer, *On Kierkegaard and the Truth*.

Kierkegaard? What did he write? What did he read? The second chapter then lays out Kierkegaard's philosophy of reading in general terms, defining the purpose of this activity in Kierkegaard's understanding. In the course of this chapter, I also briefly look at St. Augustine's theory of reading as a historical resource, demonstrating that Kierkegaard's philosophy of reading is not spontaneously generated but has deep ties to Western Christian tradition. Comparing Kierkegaard and Augustine, I show that there are broad similarities between the two; however, Kierkegaard expands the scope of an upbuilding theory of reading in ways that I argue are potentially fruitful for contemporary readers.

The next two chapters (3 and 4) focus on specific thematic accents within Kierkegaard's general philosophy of reading, namely his emphases on conceptual clarity and appropriation. These themes are defined and developed especially with reference to the prefaces of a select group of Kierkegaard's texts, including *Works of Love* and *Upbuilding Discourses in Various Spirits*. After definition of the theme in question, I highlight the reading methods Kierkegaard recommends for developing conceptual clarity and appropriation, moving from what these Kierkegaardian concerns are to how we might implement them.

Chapter 5, "Don't Read, Act!," constitutes the surprising conclusion to Kierkegaard's philosophy of reading. Ultimately, Kierkegaard wants us to stop reading and leap into action. Although reading can clarify for us what actions are the right ones to take, this clarity is of no use if it is not translated into the risks of activity. Paradoxically, then, Kierkegaard's philosophy of reading ends with a call to stop reading. As we will see, however, the contradiction apparent in this paradox is only superficial: for Kierkegaard, reading is always in service to something else. Thus it is entirely appropriate that if reading begins to get in the way of this "something else," it should be discarded.

In conclusion, I dispel the possible illusion that I consider Kierkegaard's philosophy of reading to be completely sufficient by considering what I hold to be its chief flaw, and I offer a counter to this flaw by drawing on a selected passage from the influential

Orthodox theologian St. Gregory of Nazianzus (329–390 AD).
Just because Kierkegaard's philosophy of reading has flaws does
not mean we have nothing to learn from it, however. Over the
course of the next few chapters, I hope to show that we stand in Kierkegaard's debt: there is an abundance of wisdom still to discover
in the "melancholy Dane," including the significant gift he gives us
of increasing our understanding of why we in fact should do this
activity which many of us spend so much time doing.

Acknowledgments

In 2016, I HAD the immense privilege of taking a class on Kierkegaard's spiritual writings with C. Stephen Evans. This class was the origin for my interest in Kierkegaard's philosophy of reading, and Professor Evans encouraged that interest, causing it to grow into the obsession it became. That this book exists is a testament to Professor Evans's skill as a mentor for young scholars of Kierkegaard. To him, I am profoundly grateful.

Kim Paffenroth invited me to contribute an earlier version of Chapter 2 to *Augustine and Kierkegaard*, part of the Augustine in Conversation series. Thank you, Kim.

I must also thank Paul Martens, the first person in my life who told me I could be a scholar. For his continuing support and guidance, I am constantly in need of giving more thanks than I am able.

There are many "Kierkegaard friends" to mention as well. Eleanor, Adam, Koa, Jeff, Carl, Mariana, Tony, Tomer, Troy, Wojtek, Sylvia, Marcia, and Lee: I am so lucky to have you as companions along this peculiar way.

Finally, a huge thanks to Gordon Marino for inviting me to be a Senior Research Fellow at the Hong Kierkegaard Library, St. Olaf College, for the 2019–2020 year. To him and to all the people who make the library possible, tusind tak!

Abbreviations

CA   *The Concept of Anxiety: A Simple Psychologically Orient-*
      ing Deliberation on the Dogmatic Issue of Hereditary Sin,
      edited and translated by Reidar Thomte, in collabora-
      tion with Albert B. Anderson, Kierkegaard's Writings,
      vol. VIII. Princeton, NJ: Princeton University Press,
      1980.

CI   *The Concept of Irony, with Continual Reference to*
      Socrates; Notes of Schelling's Berlin Lectures, edited and
      translated by Howard V. Hong and Edna H. Hong, Ki-
      erkegaard's Writings, vol. II. Princeton, NJ: Princeton
      University Press, 1989.

COR   *The Corsair Affair and Articles Related to the Writings*,
      edited and translated by Howard V. Hong and Edna H.
      Hong, Kierkegaard's Writings, vol. XIII. Princeton, NJ:
      Princeton University Press, 1982.

CUP   *Concluding Unscientific Postscript to Philosophical Frag-*
      ments, Volume I: Text, edited and translated by Howard
      V. Hong and Edna H. Hong, Kierkegaard's Writings, vol.
      XII:1. Princeton, NJ: Princeton University Press, 1992.

EOI   *Either/Or, Part I*, edited and translated by Howard V.
      Hong and Edna H. Hong, Kierkegaard's Writings, vol.
      III. Princeton, NJ: Princeton University Press, 1987.

EOII   *Either/Or, Part II*, edited and translated by Howard V. Hong and Edna H. Hong, Kierkegaard's Writings, vol. IV. Princeton, NJ: Princeton University Press, 1987.

EUD   *Eighteen Upbuilding Discourses*, edited and translated by Howard V. Hong and Edna H. Hong, Kierkegaard's Writings, vol. V. Princeton, NJ: Princeton University Press, 1990.

FSE   *For Self-Examination*, in *For Self-Examination; Judge for Yourself!*, edited and translated by Howard V. Hong and Edna H. Hong, Kierkegaard's Writings, vol. XXI. Princeton, NJ: Princeton University Press, 1990.

FT   *Fear and Trembling*, in *Fear and Trembling; Repetition*, edited and translated by Howard V. Hong and Edna H. Hong, Kierkegaard's Writings, vol. VI. Princeton, NJ: Princeton University Press, 1983.

IKC   *International Kierkegaard Commentary*, edited by Robert L. Perkins, vols. 1–24. Macon, GA: Mercer University Press, 1984–2010.

JP   *Søren Kierkegaard's Journals and Papers*, edited and translated by Howard V. Hong and Edna H. Hong, assisted by Gregor Malantschuk, vols. 1–6. Bloomington, IN: Indiana University Press, 1967–1978.

KJN   *Kierkegaard's Journals and Notebooks*, edited by Niels Jørgen Cappelørn, Alastair Hannay, David Kangas, Bruce H. Kirmmse, George Pattison, Vanessa Rumble, and K. Brian Söderquist, vols. 1–11. Princeton, NJ: Princeton University Press, 2007ff.

KRSRR *Kierkegaard Research: Sources, Reception and Resources*, edited by Jon Stewart, vols. 1–21. Aldershot: Ashgate; London: Routledge, 2007–2017.

KSYB   *Kierkegaard Studies Yearbook*, Years 1998–2018, edited by Niels Jørgen Cappeljørn, et al. Berlin: Walter de Gruyter, 1998ff.

LR   *Two Ages: The Age of Revolution and the Present Age*, edited and translated by Howard V. Hong and Edna H. Hong, Kierkegaard's Writings, vol. XIV. Princeton, NJ: Princeton University Press, 1978.

Pap.   *Søren Kierkegaards Papirer*, edited by P. A. Heiberg, V. Kuhr, and E. Torsting, vols. I–XI-3. Copenhagen: Gyldendal, 1909–1948.

PC   *Practice in Christianity*, edited and translated by Howard V. Hong and Edna H. Hong, Kierkegaard's Writings, vol. XX. Princeton, NJ: Princeton University Press, 1991.

PF   *Philosophical Fragments*, edited and translated by Howard V. Hong and Edna H. Hong, Kierkegaard's Writings, vol. VII. Princeton, NJ: Princeton University Press, 1998.

PV   *The Point of View: On My Work as an Author; The Point of View for My Work as an Author; Armed Neutrality*, edited and translated by Howard V. Hong and Edna H. Hong, Kierkegaard's Writings, vol. XXII. Princeton, NJ: Princeton University Press, 1998.

SKS   *Søren Kierkegaards Skrifter*, ed. Niels Jørgen Cappelørn, Joakim Garff, Jette Knudsen, and Johnny Kondrup, vols. 1–28, K1–K28. Copenhagen: Gads Forlag, 1997–2013.

SUD   *The Sickness unto Death: A Christian Psychological Exposition for Upbuilding and Awakening*, edited and translated by Howard V. Hong and Edna H. Hong, Kierkegaard's Writings, vol. XIX. Princeton, NJ: Princeton University Press, 1980.

TM   *The Moment and Late Writings*, edited and translated by Howard V. Hong and Edna H. Hong, Kierkegaard's Writings, vol. XXIII. Princeton, NJ: Princeton University Press, 1998.

UDVS   *Upbuilding Discourses in Various Spirits*, edited and translated by Howard V. Hong and Edna H. Hong,

Kierkegaard's Writings, vol. XV. Princeton, NJ: Princeton University Press, 1993.

WL   *Works of Love*, edited and translated by Howard V. Hong and Edna H. Hong, Kierkegaard's Writings, vol. XVI. Princeton, NJ: Princeton University Press, 1995.

A Note on Citation

WHEN REFERRING TO KIERKEGAARD'S published writings, I first make reference to the English translation in the Kierkegaard's Writings series (with the appropriate abbreviation, listed above), followed by its cross-reference in the Danish critical edition (*SKS*) with the appropriate volume number. For example: *TM*, 190 / *SKS* 13, 241. When referring to Kierkegaard's unpublished journal writings, I first make reference to the English translation in the *Kierkegaard's Journals and Notebooks* series (*KJN*), with the appropriate volume number, followed by its cross-reference in the Danish critical edition (*SKS*), with the appropriate volume number, followed by the journal entry number. For example: *KJN* 4, 373–375 / *SKS* 20, 373–375, NB5:10. On occasion I will cite a journal entry from the Hongs' translation (*JP*); in these cases, I refer to the entry number (e.g., *JP* 5007).

1 Kierkegaard's Life, Writings, and Readings

THIS CHAPTER IS INTENDED to be both a general introduction to Kierkegaard and a specific introduction to this book. I answer three questions: Who was Kierkegaard? What did he write? What did he read?

Kierkegaard's life spanned the years 1813 to 1855, placing him right in the middle of Golden Age Denmark.[1] This period in Denmark's history is notable for its recovering economy, after a crash in 1813 (though it should be noted that this recovery relied upon exploitation of the labor of Denmark's colonies). This economic underpinning supported a flourishing cultural renaissance, with respect to everything from politics, drama, philosophy, and science, to literature, theology, and painting.[2] In 1848, a seemingly major shift happened in Danish politics, as Denmark transitioned from an absolute to a constitutional monarchy. However, the fact that this transition happened without violence and really did not

---

1. Kirmmse's *Kierkegaard in Golden Age Denmark* remains an outstanding reference, with full chapters devoted to several of the most important figures of the Danish Golden Age.

2. Among the many possible references here, there is a lovely book on Danish painting: Berman's *In Another Light*.

change all that much is emblematic of the period. Excepting the excluded,[3] this was a period of happy comfort and bourgeois virtue.

Søren Kierkegaard was born to a family wealthy enough to facilitate a full and leisured engagement with the many cultural resources of the Danish Golden Age.[4] His father, Michael Pedersen Kierkegaard, not only made a fortune as a clothing merchant; he also shrewdly invested this fortune in "so-called royal obligations" or bonds before Denmark's currency collapsed as a result of the aforementioned economic catastrophe.[5] With his own fortune secure as so many others were devalued, in the aftermath of the crash M. P. Kierkegaard was one of the wealthiest men in Denmark.

The wealth accrued by the elder Kierkegaard supported Søren throughout his life. After growing up in a house on Nyrtov, near the center of Copenhagen, Kierkegaard attended the University of Copenhagen and took many years to finish his degree. During this extended time at university, Kierkegaard lived as a flâneur or dandy,[6] wearing expensive clothes, participating in elite literary salons, frequenting the opera and the theatre, drinking strong coffee at costly cafés, and generally running up large debts which his father had to pay off.

After living this relatively dissolute life for some time, Kierkegaard fell in love. The woman's name was Regine Olsen, whom Kierkegaard met in 1837. She was charming, intelligent, and eight years Kierkegaard's junior. It was an intense romance, beginning

3. During this time period, the excluded were principally the cottagers and the colonies. On the cottagers or "landless and often aged and infirm rural day laborers," see Kirmmse, *Kierkegaard in Golden Age Denmark*, 14–19 (the above quote is excerpted from 14). On the colonies, see Pedersen et al., *Danmark og kolonierne*, 5 volumes; my thanks to Nigel Hatton for pointing me to this reference.

4. I rely on three excellent biographies for the details in what follows. For a vast, comprehensive yet still entertaining treatment of Kierkegaard's life, see Garff, *Søren Aabye Kierkegaard*. For a quick overview that reads like a well-written novel, see Backhouse, *Kierkegaard*. For a concise lyrical, poetic, and philosophic treatment of Kierkegaard's life and writings, see Carlisle, *Philosopher of the Heart*.

5. See Garff, *Søren Aabye Kierkegaard*, 8.

6. For a classic definition, see Baudelaire, *The Painter of Modern Life*, 9–12.

with Kierkegaard throwing sheets of music onto the floor as he declared his passion. But the romance was just as intense in its end as in its beginning. On August 11, 1841, Kierkegaard sent his engagement ring back to Regine. She was distraught; Copenhagen was a small enough place that all the society with which Regine was familiar would soon know of her broken engagement.

Regine pleaded with Kierkegaard, but he remained resolute in his decision. Though we can't know for sure (since we must rely on Kierkegaard's own account), it is likely Kierkegaard broke off the engagement for two reasons: (1) he recognized he had an incurable melancholy, knew its deleterious effects, and did not want to make another person suffer through this condition with him (Regine, on the other hand, was of a rather sunny disposition); (2) he understood himself as called by God to be an author, and considered marriage incompatible with this vocation.[7]

Kierkegaard did in fact soon become an author. He took a trip to Berlin shortly after breaking off his engagement to Regine, and there he wrote the majority of his first real published book, *Either/Or* (1843).[8]

Kierkegaard's first book was also one of his most successful. It was one of his only writings to sell out and receive a second printing. *Either/Or* is a collection of diverse material, from short philosophic-melancholic aphorisms to a treatise on Mozart and a long defense of marriage as a pleasurable institution. What makes the book unique is not just the obvious genius of its author, but two complicating factors in addition: (1) the book's authorship is not ascribed to Kierkegaard, but to various pseudonyms, who are not simple noms de plume but imaginary characters created by Kierkegaard; (2) Kierkegaard released a pair of religious writings

---

7. Though we will follow Kierkegaard's life from this point, the rest of Regine's story is told in Garff's excellent *Kierkegaard's Muse*.

8. Kierkegaard had published an earlier volume in book format, titled *From the Papers of One Still Living*. However, this earlier publication was more of an extended book review than a book in its own right, and Kierkegaard does not include the text as part of his authorship proper in *The Point of View* (a kind of retrospective on his work authored by Kierkegaard himself).

at nearly the same time as the aesthetical-ethical *Either/Or*, and to these writings he affixed his own name.

Right from the start, Kierkegaard's authorship resisted any simple interpretation. Was he a religious author encouraging his readers to embrace the eternal God as the giver of all good gifts? Or was he an aesthete, penning tracts on how to best drain this world of all the pleasure it can give? Or was he a bourgeois apologist, extolling the inherent beauty of the ordinary married life of upstanding Danish citizens? It wasn't clear to his original audience exactly which of these things Kierkegaard was, and the ambiguity is intentional. Kierkegaard wanted to block any easy identification of the "message" of his writings, leaving the reader unmoored enough that she must grapple with what, considering multiple options, *she* thinks the truth to be. There is thus a kind of self-activity required of Kierkegaard's readers that not every author demands.

Over the span of the next ten years, Kierkegaard would continue this diverse production of writings, and at a rapid pace, often publishing several lengthy volumes in the same year. The texts cover a range of topics, from a religious critique of bourgeois morality (*Fear and Trembling*, 1843) to a psychological treatment of original sin (*The Concept of Anxiety*, 1843), a foundational text in existential philosophy (*Concluding Unscientific Postscript*, 1846), and a profound exploration of the spiritual phenomenon of despair (*The Sickness unto Death*, 1849).

During all this time of intense productivity, Kierkegaard lived an otherwise uneventful life. He mainly spent his time walking around the city of Copenhagen, talking to any and every one. Kierkegaard was Copenhagen's greatest peripatetic,[9] and the daily conversations he had—in which he "pumped" his conversation partners for their views and opinions on different topics—served as fodder for the books he was so rapidly writing.[10] After publication of *Concluding Unscientific Postscript* in 1846, and especially after being attacked by the satirical newspaper *The Corsair* in 1846 and 1847, Kierkegaard's authorship grew more distinctly religious

9. See Christensen, *Peripatetikeren Søren Kierkegaard*, 5.
10. See Kirmmse, ed., *Encounters with Kierkegaard*, 91, 95–96.

in character, though he would still publish the occasional aesthetic piece, such as his fascinating theatre review, "The Crisis and a Crisis in the Life of an Actress" (1848).

Eventually, with the publication of *For Self-Examination* in September of 1851, Kierkegaard's pen fell silent—at least for a while. When he began publishing again on December 18, 1854, he spoke openly in a newspaper article about judgments he had held in secret for a long time: namely, that the Danish State Church was hopelessly corrupt and actually prevented the cultivation of Christianity rather than aiding its development.

The "Attack upon Christendom," as this article and those that followed have come to be called, is notable within the context of Kierkegaard's authorship for two principal reasons. (1) Its rhetorical exaggeration. Kierkegaard calls pastors cannibals, child-bearing a sin, and contends that the only true Christian is a martyr whose body has been "crucified or beheaded or burned or broiled on a grill."[11] This rhetoric was employed in an effort to shock his audience, to get their blood stirring.[12] (2) Its intended effect. Throughout his authorship, Kierkegaard writes to produce what he calls "inward deepening."[13] The "Attack" literature is still concerned with this project, but it also wants to have a larger, more structural effect on religion in Denmark. Kierkegaard really hopes his writing will lead to the downfall of the State Church, with people voluntarily opting out of church attendance, resulting in the waning of the State Church as an institution. In this way, Kierkegaard is offering his own version of a public or political theology, proposing that if the Danish State and the Danish State Church's twofold project is to make Denmark's citizens comfortable in this life and the next, then true Christianity can have no part in it. This might seem curmudgeonly, but Kierkegaard believed the comforts of the world were necessarily achieved by evil means, and now

11. *TM*, 6 / *SKS* 14, 125.

12. Ibid., 12 / 131: "Therefore an objection should be raised, and then as emphatically as possible the blood should be stirred, passion set in motion."

13. The locus classicus is *CUP* Part Two, Chapter Two, "Subjective Truth, Inwardness; Truth Is Subjectivity," 189–251 / *SKS* 7, 173–273.

that we know more about the history of Danish colonialism and the true cost of the bourgeois Danish citizen's comfort, it appears Kierkegaard may be correct.[14]

In the midst of his attack on the church, Kierkegaard grew seriously ill, collapsing in the middle of September, 1855, and being taken to Frederick's Hospital, where, some weeks later, he died.[15] By that point, he had authored some thirty books in genres as diverse as philosophy, theology, spiritual literature, psychology, and literary criticism. During the course of all these writings, Kierkegaard also developed a cogent and useful philosophy of reading, the subject of the current book.

Kierkegaard's own practice of reading was as diverse as his writing—in fact, even more so. Kierkegaard did read the basics for someone of a philosophical-theological bent: he was thoroughly familiar with the Scriptures, even at one point making his own translation of the New Testament from Greek into Latin. He was also immersed in ancient and modern philosophical literature, reading through Plato for his dissertation and becoming acquainted with the works of Descartes, Kant, Fichte, Hegel, Schelling, and Hamann. But beyond these two traditional locations, Kierkegaard also read quite widely, even eclectically. He did extensive research in fairy-tale literature, as well as reading in aesthetic theory, fiction, Aristotle's theory of motion, poetry, drama, and comedy (being especially well-versed in the work of Aristophanes). This eclectic practice of reading is in part why it took Kierkegaard so long to finish his preliminary exams in theology at university. He was distracted by all the different fields that held his interest.

As he grew older, Kierkegaard's reading took on two additional foci: Martin Luther and devotional literature. In 1849–1852, Kierkegaard returned to the Luther familiar to him from boyhood and found much in him that remained valuable.[16] Around the same period, Kierkegaard began reading more and more devotional

---

14. See above, n. 3.

15. See Garff, *Søren Aabye Kierkegaard*, 782.

16. See the excellent treatment of Kierkegaard's relation to Luther in Podmore, "The Lightening and the Earthquake," 562–78.

literature, especially Thomas à Kempis's *Imitation of Christ* and the writings of German and Danish Pietists such as and Johann Arndt, Gerhard Tersteegen, and Hans Adolph Brorson.[17] This literature sustained Kierkegaard through the last portion of his life, which was in general characterized by sufferings both physical and spiritual in nature.

Out of all the many things he read, Kierkegaard's favorite text was a Bible verse, James 1:17: "Every good and every perfect gift is from above and comes down from the Father of lights, with whom there is no change or shadow of variation."[18] Kierkegaard cherished this text, turning to it repeatedly in his writing and finding much comfort and solace in it. It was one text among many that Kierkegaard made fully his own.

Now that we have covered Kierkegaard's life, writings, and readings, we can turn to the central topic of this book—namely, why Kierkegaard thinks human beings should practice this art that he was so dedicated to, the art of reading.

17. For an extensive history, see Barnett, *Kierkegaard, Pietism and Holiness*, chapter 3, "Kierkegaard's Reading of Pietist Literature: An Investigation of Themes Christian and Socratic," 63–109.

18. On James 1:17 as Kierkegaard's favorite verse, see especially *JP* 6965 / *Pap.* XI 3 B 291:4, August 1855 (as it is part of a draft manuscript for "The Changelessness of God," this entry cannot be found in the *SKS* edition). Here I use the biblical translation provided in the English translation of Kierkegaard's first discourse on James 1:17–22; this translation reflects the Danish translation Kierkegaard was using at the time. See *EUD*, 32 / *SKS* 5, 41.

2 You Must Change Your Life
Kierkegaard and Augustine on Reading

WHEN WE SIT DOWN to read a book, what is it that we think we are doing? Maybe this reading is compulsory, as part of a school assignment. Or perhaps if we are older we are doing something generally considered appropriate for a scholar's life, namely gathering knowledge. On the other hand, we could be escaping scholastic duties by seeking entertainment through some illicit genre (e.g., novels). We could also be indulging nostalgia, recollecting a past we prefer to the present. Or it's possible that more is at stake: maybe we are waiting for the arrival of a presence—a voice so like our own, so sharing in fellow feeling and experience, that we no longer feel so isolated in our subjectivity.

There are, no doubt, many reasons to read a book. Considering this bewildering variety of options presses us to ask the question: is there a *right* answer to this query? Do we—or should we—consciously subscribe to any normative account of what the activity of reading should try to accomplish?

Both St. Augustine (354–430 AD) and Søren Kierkegaard thought that we should, and their answer to the question is remarkably similar. On this issue of reading, as on many others, Lee C. Barrett is right to claim that Kierkegaard and Augustine share far more than they diverge.[1] Although eventually I will get to a

---

1. An earlier version of this chapter appeared as "You Must Change Your

matter of significant disagreement, I begin with Augustine and Kierkegaard's shared answer to the question just posed; namely, whether we should subscribe to a normative account of what reading is for.

Both their answers go something like this: Reading is not just an activity we do willy-nilly, picking up a book and then seeing what happens. Rather, reading should be about the transformation of the self. We should have that specific aim in mind when we read; all other purposes, from entertainment to knowledge acquisition to nostalgia, are missing the point and should be actively and consciously refused and rejected.[2] The point of reading is to open a space wherein the self can be transformed toward greater love of God and neighbor. Reading that serves another purpose—or no definite purpose—is, quite simply, illegitimate: it is a misuse of this activity, a missing-of-the-mark for which there will need to be repentance (or *metanoia*).[3]

In order to understand why the transformation of the self is the purpose of reading for both Kierkegaard and Augustine, it is helpful to place each author's philosophy of reading within a broader context specific to his work. Thus, in the next few paragraphs I highlight a theme that is central to each respective author and then show how his philosophy of reading is connected to this theme. For Augustine, I look to his account of use and enjoyment (or *uti/frui*), before turning to the notion of writing "without authority" for Kierkegaard.

First, Augustine on *uti/frui*. Although it is a distinction Augustine brings up in several different contexts in a variety of his works,[4] the crucial location for understanding Augustine on the

---

Life: Kierkegaard and Augustine on Reading."

See especially the introductory chapter "Augustine and Kierkegaard: Rivals or Allies?" in Barrett, *Eros and Self-Emptying*, 1–25.

2. To clarify: these can be beneficial side-effects of reading, but their experience must not be its point.

3. On *metanoia*, see for example Mark 1:4: "John the baptizer appeared in the wilderness, proclaiming a baptism of repentance (μετανοίας) for the forgiveness of sins."

4. See, for example, Augustine, *City of God*, XVIII.54.

difference between use (*uti*) and enjoyment (*frui*) is the first book of his *On Teaching Christianity*, or *De Doctrina Christiana* (426 AD). In the late fourth and early fifth centuries, Augustine was the bishop of Hippo in North Africa (modern-day Annaba, Algeria). He oversaw many priests who worked in the several churches that fell under his jurisdiction as bishop. *De Doctrina Christiana* is a book whose target audience is these priests.[5] It is intended to provide instruction on how to instruct: that is, how to be a priest who leads one's congregation to a greater love of God. Of particular interest to Augustine is the art of preaching, which leads to the investigations of biblical interpretation and rhetoric that one finds throughout *De Doctrina Christiana*.

While Book Four of *De Doctrina* is devoted to rhetoric, the ostensible topic of Book One is biblical interpretation; however, many other topics are also treated. Because Augustine's discussion of use and enjoyment in the first book of *De Doctrina Christiana* ranges over such broad territory, from the Trinity to human beings to friendship to angels, it can be difficult to remember that the discussion begins and ends with the topic of reading. Augustine has a habit of writing in long thematic spirals, branching out over many issues but eventually returning to the particular occasion for the matter at hand. Thus, after beginning with the activity of reading, then spanning the whole of God and creation, Augustine near the end of the first book of *De Doctrina* returns to ask if the reading and understanding of Scripture is an end to be enjoyed in itself. In other words, is it okay to simply delight in reading the Scriptures, with no further purpose in mind? No, Augustine answers, for the reading of Scripture is not an end in itself. The purpose of reading Scripture is the cultivation of love. That Scripture is something to be used, via reading, in order to grow in love becomes most clear when Augustine discusses the possibility of interpretive error:

> So if it seems to you that you have understood the divine
> scriptures, or any part of them, in such a way that by this
> understanding you do not build up this twin love of God

5. For a fuller introduction to *De Doctrina Christiana*, see Levering, *The Theology of Augustine*, 1–18.

and neighbor, then you have not yet understood them. If on the other hand you have made judgments about them that are helpful for building up this love, but for all that have not said what the author you have been reading actually meant in that place, then your mistake is not pernicious . . .

[A]ny who understands a passage in the scriptures to mean something which the writer did not mean are mistaken . . . But all the same, as I had started to say, if they are mistaken in a judgment which is intended to build up charity, which is *the end of the law* (1 Tim. 1:5), they are mistaken in the same sort of way as people who go astray off the road, but still proceed by rough paths to the same place as the road was taking them to.[6]

Of course, it would be the ultimate ideal to be completely correct in all your interpretations *and* have those interpretations build you up into further love of God and neighbor. But if you make an incorrect interpretation of a text while still using it to build up love, "then," as Augustine says, "your mistake is not pernicious"; for in your interpretation you are still achieving the true end goal of reading: growth in love.

As at the end of Augustine's book on the Trinity, *De Trinitate*, it is clear that wisdom (*sapientia*) takes precedence over knowledge (*scientia*).[7] Reading is not so much about the pursuit of knowledge as it is growth in wisdom, with wisdom being defined as right love of God and neighbor. Scripture, and by implication any other text taken up in the human activity of reading, is something to be used for the enjoyment of God. Reading, therefore, has a clear and distinct purpose: the transformation of the self into one who enjoys God and loves the neighbor. According to Augustine, we can love texts, but we love them as "we love the means by which we are being carried along, on account of the goal to which we are being carried."[8]

6. Augustine, *De Doctrina Christiana*, I.36, 40–41; *Teaching Christianity*, 124.

7. Augustine, *De Trinitate* XV; cf. Stock, *Augustine the Reader*, 278.

8. Augustine, *De Doctrina* I.35, 39; *Teaching Christianity*, 123.

Though I have only briefly mentioned a couple of texts, this analysis of Augustine on the topic of reading is supported by the clear and extensively documented treatment in Brian Stock's 1996 book, *Augustine the Reader*. What we find in Augustine, who offers according to Stock "the West's first developed theory of reading," is a combination of "the Christian ideal of self-reform and the meditative life of the reader," such that in a proper act of reading we are lead "upward and inward" to a place where our own self cannot remain the same: it must change its life. Through reading, the self has grown in the love of God and in wisdom, and this growth will necessarily have an effect on its daily habits and decisions.[9]

When it comes to an understanding of what should happen in the activity of reading, Kierkegaard continues much the same trajectory as Augustine. He too believes that reading should fundamentally be about self-transformation. This belief lies behind one of the most oft-repeated phrases in Kierkegaard's authorship. He repeatedly insists that his writings are "without authority," a phrase that applies equally well to the signed and the pseudonymous writings—they are all the creations of a poet, a maker (*Digter*), who creatively presents ideas that the reader is free to appropriate, or not.[10]

In our postmodern context, we might think that the phrase "without authority" is endorsing moral relativism or the fundamental indeterminacy of a text's meaning. Yet nothing could be further from the case, for the idea of writing "without authority" actually presumes a normative account of what *should* be happening when the reader is reading. Kierkegaard withholds authority precisely in order to enable the reader to take up the task of self-transformation for herself. The idea of appropriation is key: writing without authority, Kierkegaard leaves space for the active

---

9. Stock, *Augustine the Reader*, 1, 17.

10. As Kierkegaard puts it in *On my Work as an Author*, "'Without authority' to make aware of the religious, the essentially Christian, is the category for my whole work as an author regarded as a totality" (*PV*, 12 / *SKS* 13, 19).

reader, that single individual who takes up an idea given by a text and puts it to work in her own life.[11]

Leaving space for free appropriation does not mean Kierkegaard has no specific goal in mind for the readers of his texts. In fact, the one whom Kierkegaard calls "my reader" is the reader who reads with a view to her life being changed as a result of this activity.[12] If this does not happen, the reader is not reading as one should, according to Kierkegaard. Only the reader who in the act of reading ends up before God is truly reading. "Without authority," then, is not a bit of postmodern ideology, but a rhetorical strategy designed to allow the reader to have her own encounter with the authority of God. Compared to Augustine, we can see that although the rhetorical strategies of the two authors are in many ways quite different, the end goal is the same.[13] What the reader should gain by reading is an increase in love and wisdom through an encounter with God.

That this is Kierkegaard's general philosophy of reading is further confirmed by what Kierkegaard has to say about reading a text that does have divine authority. In his 1851 book titled *For Self-Examination*, we see Kierkegaard dismantling various obstacles that have managed to insinuate themselves between the reader and the authority of Scripture. He accomplishes this most

---

11. *PV*, 118 / *SKS* 16, 98. I turn to the topic of appropriation in full in chapter 4.

12. "My reader": see, for example, the Preface to the two upbuilding discourses of 1843: "After a few little mistakes, through being deceived by a fleeting resemblance, it [i.e., the book itself] finally met that single individual [*hinn Enkelte*] whom I with joy and gratitude call *my* reader, that single individual it is seeking, to whom, so to speak, it stretches out its arms, that single individual who is favorably enough disposed to allow himself to be found, favorably enough disposed to receive it" (*EUD*, 5 / *SKS* 5, 13; emphasis original).

13. Barrett makes much the same point: Kierkegaard and Augustine's "selection of literary strategies was very self-conscious, for both writers wanted to move readers to think and feel more deeply rather than merely provide readers with new information, clearer concepts, or more compelling arguments"; thus both authors "were intent on catalyzing a spiritual transformation of their readers" (*Eros and Self-Emptying*, 17).

memorably through the metaphor of the love letter.[14] In this metaphor or parable, the lover receives a letter from his beloved in a foreign language, and therefore must first decipher the text with the help of a dictionary. This reader and lover will not think that during all this time spent deciphering he is actually reading the love letter. In fact, the recipient of the letter—the lover—gets quite angry when a friend suggests that he is reading the letter from his beloved when he is still deciphering it:

> "Have you gone mad?" [he exclaims] "Do you think this is reading a letter from my beloved! No, my friend, I am sitting here toiling and moiling with a dictionary to get it translated. At times I am ready to explode with impatience; the blood rushes to my head and I would just as soon hurl the dictionary on the floor—and you call that reading—you must be joking! No, thank God, I am soon finished with the translation and then, yes, then, I shall read my beloved's letter; that is something altogether different. But to whom am I speaking. . . . stupid fellow, get out of my sight; I would rather not see you—how could you think of insulting my beloved and me by calling this reading a letter from her! And yet, stay, stay—you know very well I am only joking. I would ever so much like to have you stay, but, to be honest, I have no time. There is still something left to translate and I am so impatient to begin reading it—therefore do not be angry, but please go so I can finish."[15]

All that the potential reader has done is only preparation, getting ready to read the love letter. Kierkegaard then brings the metaphor home:

> Now think of God's Word. When you read God's Word in a scholarly way—we do not disparage scholarship, no, far from it, but do bear this in mind: when you are reading God's Word in a scholarly way, with a dictionary etc., then you are not reading God's Word . . . God's Word is given in order that you shall act according to it, not that

---

14. For further treatment of the love letter metaphor, see chapter 5.

15. *FSE*, 27 / *SKS* 13, 54–55.

you shall practice interpreting obscure passages. If you do not read God's Word in such a way that you consider that the least little bit you do understand instantly binds you to do accordingly, then you are not reading God's Word.[16]

In short, chasing down every tittle and jot of Scripture that we have yet to bring within the domain of our knowledge can often be a way of avoiding the divine authority of the text. The normative dimensions of such a judgment are clear: either you are reading the text to encounter the binding Word of God, or you are not really reading God's Word. The ultimate purpose of reading Scripture, then, is to have a binding encounter with divine authority. The words of the text are to be *used* for this specific purpose, and that means they are *not* to be used for the purpose of indulging a reader's penchant for obscure knowledge (a penchant which is often just a strategy to avoid divine authority, at any rate); neither are the Scriptures to be enjoyed in themselves, as if their purpose were self-contained. No: true reading of Scripture happens when that reading places one before God.

But, as we have seen, reading Scripture is just a special case of what should happen in all reading. Scripture and the ordained pastor use one strategy—namely, the direct authority of command—while Kierkegaard uses another. Ultimately, the result should be the same: obedience to the God into whose presence the reader has come. God arrives in the text properly read.

On this fundamental point about the purpose of reading Kierkegaard and Augustine are in agreement. Kierkegaard's philosophy of reading therefore in many ways continues Augustine's legacy, whether he is aware of that fact or not. Agreement about the fundamental purpose of reading doesn't, however, mean that Kierkegaard and Augustine agree on everything. Augustine is much more comfortable with seeing contemplation as an end-goal for reading, for example, while Kierkegaard seems to want reading always to end in action.

16. *FSE*, 29 / *SKS* 13, 56–57.

There is another difference, however, that I would like to focus on and tease out. It has to do with what sort of reading material can serve the purpose of reading as Kierkegaard and Augustine imagine it. Although he retains a constant ambivalence about the matter, never forthrightly condemning the reading of pagan poetic literature, the trajectory of Augustine's autobiographical *Confessions* is clear: he goes from reading Virgil and attending the theater to reading Cicero and, ultimately, the Scriptures. Philosophy and Scripture are given clear priority as material for the reading life of the reader who reads in order to encounter God.

Kierkegaard does not limit his reading material in this fashion. In fact, in one of the most interesting and least explored passages in Kierkegaard's corpus, he provides a stirring defense for the spiritual value of reading fiction. *A Literary Review*, otherwise known as *Two Ages*, has largely received attention on account of its depictions of the present age and the levelling process that seem so close to Martin Heidegger's description of *das Man* (or "the they").[17] The "Introduction" to his literary review of Thomasine Gyllembourg's *A Story of Everyday Life*, on the other hand, is often overlooked. Yet it is here that Kierkegaard provides something unexpected: an extended commentary on how reading novels, particularly novels written with what Kierkegaard calls a coherent "life-view,"[18] can contribute to the process of self-transformation. Let us pause a moment, then, to consider why and how Kierkegaard thinks novels are suitable reading material for placing us before God.

Kierkegaard proposes that what the author of *A Story of Everyday Life* displays in her novels is a coherent life-view, a life-view that "lies on the boundary of the esthetic and in the direction of the religious."[19] Situating Gyllembourg's novel in this ambiguous space is key, for what novels with this type of life-view do is take the everyday pleasures and pains of life (the esthetic) and show how they can be infused with religious knowledge. When this

17. For a representative sample, see the essays collected in *IKC* 14.

18. *LR*, 14–19 / *SKS* 8, 17–22.

19. Ibid., 14 / 18.

religious knowledge meets our everyday esthetic life, it enables a certain kind of resigned acceptance to fate or Governance that is key to the ethical life of the self, a life which is characterized by continuity over time.

In other words, the continuity characteristic of the ethical life of the self is dependent upon a series of attitudes the individual develops in inwardness, attitudes which assist in dealing with the vicissitudes of temporal life, including: common sense, patience, friendly sympathy, contentment, and resignation. These attitudes are all infused with a "religious tinge," or the knowledge that this life is not all there is.[20] One is able to adopt the attitudes necessary to ethical life as a result of the awareness that one's everyday life is set within a broader context of meaning and final wholeness. Resignation to a lamentable and ineradicable fact of one's life—such as the death of a loved one or a chronic illness—is impossible apart from this greater religious context, wherein we see that it is God who has given us all the pains and pleasures of our everyday lives, that we can relate to God in inwardness through them, and that God—who is all eyes[21]—sees and remembers what happens to us, and will reward us accordingly. Gyllembourg's novels help us stay at our station, remain at our post, and grow in the love of God and neighbor as we do so.

Like Scripture and sermons, novels can place us in the presence of God in such a way that our life is changed. What is particular to the novel, however, is that—unlike an authoritative sermon that gives commands—it can lead the patient reader into its own life-view via the subtler tool of persuasion. Kierkegaard develops this theory about narratival persuasion in a paragraph that answers the question of what pedagogical means the novel uses to teach its readers that "All will be well again":

> By what means [does the novel teach this]? By using common sense so as to see a more merciful aspect of the suffering, by having the patience that expects good

---

20. Ibid., 21 / 23.

21. See *TM*, 273–78 / *SKS* 13, 332–336; cf. Martens and Millay, "Kierkegaard's Final Theodicy."

fortune to smile once again, by the friendly sympathy of loving people, by the resignation that gives up—not everything, but the highest—and by the contentment that changes the next best into something just as good as the highest. And all this is not discussed—it just happens— and for that reason the persuasiveness is so great if one gives oneself to it. No orator can be as persuasive as this, for the very reason that he has a motive, and contemplation always gives birth to doubt. But here persuasion is not a matter between two people but is the path in the life-view, and the novel leads one into the world that the view creatively supports. But this world, as a matter of fact, is actuality; thus one has not been deceived but simply has been persuaded to remain where one is.[22]

The ethical person is the one who remains at his or her station in society even in difficult times, convinced that "[a]ll will be well again." Reading novels can accomplish this convincing that is so necessary to the ethical life: as the events of the story unfold, the reader is given a greater context for whatever pain she may be experiencing, allowing her individual experience to be put in a perspective that mitigates the pain at hand. This is how novels can be, as Kierkegaard calls them, a "place of prayer."[23] Through novels, we are able to gain an inward repose about the outward events of our lives, thereby gaining the sustenance that the ethical life of the self requires.[24]

Augustine is not convinced that lasting value can arise from transient fictions.[25] Kierkegaard, on the other hand—as we have

22. *LR*, 19–20 / *SKS* 8, 22–23.

23. *LR*, 21 / *SKS* 8, 23.

24. This is not to say that remaining at one's ethical post is the be-all-end-all of the religious life for Kierkegaard; indeed, the reader may be called out of the ethical into the suffering life of a truth-witness. At that point, reading the New Testament may be more beneficial than reading novels. It should be noted, then, that what Kierkegaard develops in the "Introduction" to *A Literary Review* is not an absolute recommendation for every reader, but a development of the relative worth of novels for a reader in a particular life-situation. My thanks to Lee Barrett for bringing this needed clarification to light.

25. See Stock, *Augustine the Reader*, 36.

seen—holds that the fictive drama of novels can provide material for self-transformation that other genres of writing cannot—or at least cannot as effectively—convey. Reading a fictional narrative can indeed, according to Kierkegaard, change our lives.

In comparison with Augustine, what Kierkegaard does with his philosophy of reading should not be seen as a redefinition of the end goal of reading. Rather, Kierkegaard expands the range of material that can serve the spiritual purpose of reading. On the topic of reading, therefore, Kierkegaard continues the trajectory established in Augustine, even though he takes that trajectory further, into poetic genres of which Augustine was wary. He does not do so lightly; in fact, as we have seen, Kierkegaard undertakes significant work in order to show how novels fit into the purpose of reading as both he and Augustine understood it. This matter of disagreement about fictional narratives, then, has only demonstrated to a greater degree the fundamental agreement between Augustine and Kierkegaard on what the activity of reading is for. To those of us who read for entertainment, knowledge acquisition, or who simply don't have a conscious goal for our activity of reading, Kierkegaard and Augustine have a simple message: reading is an activity that has been granted us in order that our lives might be changed. To approach it otherwise is to approach it wrongly.

3 Conceptual Clarity

IN THE PAST, SØREN Kierkegaard has occasionally been characterized as an irrationalist.[1] Such a word suggests that reason and concepts are not valued by Kierkegaard, who—in this view—holds only to a pure faith in God's command. Such an interpretation has waned in popularity recently, principally because it is easily falsifiable. In several locations throughout his authorship, Kierkegaard speaks to the importance of concepts, even proposing that some instances of conceptual clarity are essential components of the Christian life.

Kierkegaard's high valuation of concepts is related to why he thinks reading is important, because one of the things reading can do is help increase your proficiency in the use of concepts, especially through the cultivation of conceptual clarity.

A passage from Kierkegaard's 1847 book *Works of Love* can help us begin to grasp the importance of conceptual clarity for Kierkegaard, and how the achievement of clarity is related to reading. In the Preface to the book, Kierkegaard writes: "These Christian deliberations, which are the fruit of much deliberation, will be understood slowly but then also easily."[2] For the diligent reader of Kierkegaard's journals, this—the first sentence of *Works*

---

1. See the discussion in Evans, "Is Kierkegaard an Irrationalist?" and the literature referenced therein.

2. *WL*, 3 / *SKS* 9, 11.

of Love—will have already been enough to signify that conceptual clarity will be a paramount concern of the text. That is because Kierkegaard defines the word "deliberations" (*Overveielser*) in his journals:

> A deliberation [*En Overveielse*] does not presuppose conceptual definitions as given and understood; therefore, it must not so much touch, relieve, [and] convince, as *awaken* and prod ppl. and sharpen their thinking. The moment of deliberation is thus prior to action[.][3]

Here we have a definition of "deliberation," specifically in regard to its purpose. We already know from this initial statement that a deliberation has to do with definitions. But we do not yet have specificity as to how a deliberation works or why it is important. For that we have to turn to the final few sentences of this journal entry:

> An upbuilding discourse on love presupposes that ppl. essentially know what love is, and it then seeks to win them over to love, to move them. But this is truly not the case [here].[4] Therefore the "deliberation" must first haul them up out of the cellar, call to them, turn their comfortable way of thinking upside down, with the dialectic of truth.[5]

In this passage, Kierkegaard makes an important distinction between an upbuilding discourse (*en opbyggelig Tale*) and a deliberation (*en Overveielse*). The key difference has to do with whether one believes the reader already has an adequate conceptual understanding of the matter at hand.

Kierkegaard in fact wrote many pieces that assume the reader essentially understands what is being discussed. For instance, when he writes about expectancy in "The Expectancy of Faith" and patience in "To Gain One's Soul in Patience," Kierkegaard does not define these concepts, but goes about trying to inspire his readers

---

3. *KJN* 4, 210 / *SKS* 20, 211, NB2:176.

4. I.e., the assumption that people know what "love" is.

5. *KJN* 4, 210 / *SKS* 20, 211, NB2:176; translation modified, cf. *JP* 641.

to a further existential embrace of a matter already intellectually understood.[6] But when it comes to love, Kierkegaard does not believe the reader essentially understands what he is talking about. Some form of conceptual confusion has set in, and the definition of the term has been muddied. Because of this, Kierkegaard believes a different type of writing is necessary. Instead of an upbuilding discourse, he will write a deliberation, and the goal of the latter type of writing is conceptual clarification. Love is not well understood, in Kierkegaard's opinion, so he has decided to do his part in clarifying the matter; his task as the author of *Works of Love* is therefore the clearing up of concepts.

In order for this to be Kierkegaard's task in *Works of Love*, he must as an author be operating on (at least) two assumptions: (1) conceptual clarity is a matter of some importance, its achievement being significant enough to dedicate some 400 pages to it; and (2) one of the things that reading can give the reader is conceptual clarity. If these were not the case, the task of a long written "deliberation" would be void of purpose.

Within its overall purpose of upbuilding, Kierkegaard therefore believes reading can also have this subsidiary purpose of contributing to conceptual clarity. To further grasp the importance of clarity and how it ultimately serves an upbuilding purpose, we need to look at the details of how *Works of Love* goes about its deliberative activity.

What Kierkegaard most wants to get clear about in *Works of Love* is a distinction between two concepts. Love is not one thing, according to Kierkegaard.[7] Instead, there are two categories of love, and we must learn how to distinguish them if we are really going to understand love. These two categories are *Elskov* (romantic love) and *Kjerlighed* (agapic love). The opposition between these two categories is laid out on page 52:

---

6. See *EUD* 7–29, 159–75 / *SKS* 5, 15–37, 159–74.

7. It may be Kierkegaard (or, perhaps and relatedly, Anders Nygren) that von Balthasar is contradicting when he writes in *Heart of the World*, "There are not two sorts of love" (40).

> Romantic love (*Elskov*) and friendship (*Venskab*) are
> preferential love and the passion of preferential love;
> Christian love (*Kjerlighed*) is self-denial's love, for which
> this *shall* vouches.[8]

What "preference" and "self-denial" mean are then further defined
on page 56:

> [R]omantic love and friendship are the very peak of self-
> esteem, the *I* intoxicated in the *other I*. The more securely
> one *I* and another *I* join to become one *I*, the more this
> united *I* selfishly cuts itself off from everyone else. At the
> peak of romantic love and friendship, the two actually do
> become one self, one *I*. This is explainable only because
> in preferential love there is a natural determinant (drive,
> inclination) and self-love, which selfishly can unite the
> two in a new selfish self. The spirit's love, in contrast,
> takes away from myself all natural determinants and all
> self-love.[9]

Say it is the first day of the semester. Walking into the class-
room, you see someone with rich, dark hair. They turn around
when you walk in, and their eyes are engaging, intelligent, and full
of openness to encountering you. So you go and sit by this person.
It turns out you share some interests in common, such as a love
for existential philosophy and an affinity for retro early aughts TV
dramas like *One Tree Hill*.

This sort of interaction doesn't happen all the time, and it's
exciting when it does. Sometimes you just get along with someone,
and it's no use questioning the origin of the attraction; it just happens, and the knowledge that it is happening is immediate and
intuitive.

---

8. *WL*, 52 / *SKS* 9, 59, translation modified and de-italicized. I have modified the translation of *Elskov* from "erotic love" in the Hongs' translation to
"romantic love" in the above and subsequent quotes as a result of Carl Hughes's
persuasive argument in *Kierkegaard and the Staging of Desire*, 25, 29–31.

9. *WL*, 56, / *SKS* 9, 62–63, translation modified.

This is what Aristotle meant by friendship (*philia*), and it is what Kierkegaard means by romantic love (*Elskov*).[10] Romantic love is not necessarily sexual in nature. It simply labels those situations when you have a natural affinity for another person—you enjoy being in her or his presence and you seek such presence out. Given a room full of people, you have a preference for *this* person, and such selectivity is perfectly natural.

What Kierkegaard wants to clarify is that, although *Elskov* may be natural, it is not Christian. In Kierkegaard's mind, Christian love is love that is based off Christ's command—you *shall* love your neighbor—rather than a natural attraction to the person in question. This kind of command-based love is also known as "unconditional" love. That word *unconditional* refers to the lack of conditions that need to be met before love is offered. The neighbor should not have to be pleasing to me in order for me to offer my love to him. He should not have to have a ruddy complexion, like David; nor should he have to like the same music as me, have the same political affiliations, or the same delight in witty conversation. Instead, as a Christian, I should just love him, regardless of whether he fulfills any of my preferences for the kind of person I like to be around. Christian love is love given out of obedience, not inclination.

When love is given out of obedience and not inclination, a change occurs not only in the application of love's gifts (they are now given to everyone, at all times, universally); there is also a change in the very nature of the gift of love itself. That is to say: *Kjerlighed*-type love is fundamentally different in kind from the *Elskov*-type.

In Kierkegaard's opinion, love that is based in natural inclination is actually a kind of self-love. What we like about the other is either what we like about ourselves or what we—secretly or not so secretly—wish ourselves to be. Thus, "romantic love and friendship are the very peak of self-esteem, the *I* intoxicated in the *other*

10. Here I equate romantic love (*Elskov*) and friendship (*Venskab*). According to Kierkegaard the two are closely knit, given their common basis in preference. See their synonymous status in the previous two quotations.

I.[11] At its core, romantic love (*Elskov*) is self-love; it is an affirmation of one's self and one's unique preferences, a saying "yes" to oneself as the good.[12] This can happen in traditionally romantic-sexual relationships, like Romeo and Juliet, Troilus and Cressida, Tom and Meg. Or it can happen in friendships, such as Augustine's famous-yet-unnamed companion in Book IV of the *Confessions*, a companionship he speaks about as "a very sweet experience, welded by the fervour of our identical interests,"[13] an experience which eventually causes Augustine unbearable grief when his friend is violently wrenched away from him by the merciless hand of death.

Juxtaposed to romantic love, Christian love is quite different—even opposite—in nature: "in preferential love there is a natural determinant (drive, inclination) and self-love, which selfishly can unite the two in a new selfish self. The spirit's love, by contrast, takes away from myself all natural determinants and all self-love."[14] And when "natural determinants" and "self-love" are taken away from love, it has the chance to become something more than self-serving affirmation. It has the chance to become about God:

> Worldly wisdom is of the opinion that love is a relationship between persons; Christianity teaches that love is a relationship between: a person—God—a person, that is, that God is the middle term. However beautiful a relationship of love has been between two people or among many, however complete all their desire and all their bliss have been for themselves in mutual sacrifice and devotion, even though everyone has praised this relationship—if God and the relationship have been omitted, then this, in the Christian sense, has not been love but a mutually enchanting defraudation of love. *To love God is to love oneself truly; to help another person to love God is*

11. *WL*, 56 / *SKS* 9, 62.

12. On "affirmation," see especially Deleuze, *Nietzsche and Philosophy*.

13. Augustine, *Confessions*, IV. iv (7), 56.

14. *WL*, 56 / *SKS* 9, 63.

to love another person; to be helped by another person to love God is to be loved.[15]

This is the highest calling of human love and its great dignity: that it can lead others to fulfill their own highest calling; namely, loving God. As people made in the image of God, loving God is the most exciting and fulfilling thing that we can do. The fact that we can participate in helping someone else do this should thus be an awe-inspiring reality. And it is all made possible by a love born of "self-denial,"[16] denial of the self's natural inclinations such that a reality that transcends the self can shine through. There is an Other to our world who compels love no matter what our natural inclination might be. That Other comes to presence in our world when we follow this compelling. Truly, works of *Kjerlighed* are a high calling for that mix of dust and breath called "the human being," for our works bring God into the world.

And, lest we forget, such works should be labeled "Christian." This name is doing important conceptual labor here. The presumption is that Christians should act as Christians; Christians become Christians in the doing of Christian acts. But how do we know what a "Christian act" is? Presumably, we must be able to distinguish between Christian and non-Christian acts. This is where conceptual clarity plays an important role. Giving Christian and non-Christian acts precise definitions that clearly mark out the difference between them enables the separation of the non-Christian from the Christian, which then gives the individual the ability to choose to act Christianly. It does not mean that the individual will do so, but she is at least aware of the stakes; she *can* choose the Christian, even if she does not. And, without such a capacity to choose, we cannot choose to be Christian, because we wouldn't even have the notion that there is such a choice to be made.

In a rather dramatic sense, then, Christian life depends upon conceptual clarity. Kierkegaard recognizes this, and it is why he

15. *WL*, 106–107 / *SKS* 9, 111; italics from the first sentence have been removed, while italics from the last sentence are present in the original.

16. Ibid., 4 / 12; translation modified.

writes the series of "deliberations" that together compose *Works of Love*. In distinguishing between *Elskov* and *Kjerlighed*, and giving each precise definition, Kierkegaard hopes to make the choice of Christian love a possibility.

This is what reading can do. It cannot make you a Christian, but it can—through conceptual clarity—make being a Christian possible. Something like a liberal arts education is important, then, not least because the reader is liberated to make choices that were perhaps not even available as choices before the reading of the text made the options evident as options.

Reading can therefore introduce new conceptual distinctions that shape how readers live their lives; after reading *Works of Love*, we can now choose to love in a *Kjerlighed*-type way, loving the other without condition and always keeping the other's God-relation in mind.

Yet at this point it is important to pause and prevent a possible misunderstanding. It is not as if readers are a blank slate, lacking any conception of love (for example) before the reading of a text. Reading does not write conceptual distinctions on a *tabula rasa*. Things are instead like this: first, there was conceptual confusion, and now—after reading—there is conceptual clarity. First there was a hazy, confused idea of love; now, after reading, there are clear distinctions between love and love. The different conceptual categories of love do their luminous work by clearing up the preceding fog.

Kierkegaard reflects on this shift from conceptual confusion to conceptual clarity—and what forces might prevent such a transition—in another of his books, a magnum opus of existential philosophy titled *Concluding Unscientific Postscript* (1846). Here Kierkegaard (*via* his pseudonym Johannes Climacus) proposes that conceptual confusion is no accident. Instead, it is the product of a comfortable culture that has an almost instinctual allergy to conceptual clarity.[17] Let's put it this way: if you aren't aware of a distinction between *Elskov* and *Kjerlighed*, you never have to choose between the two. And this—not having to make a choice—is easier

17. See further Millay, "Conceptual Clarity."

than facing the difficulty of decision. It is easier to accept that one has been born into a Christian country and is therefore a Christian than to interrogate one's actions according to conceptual categories that can adjudicate whether these actions are Christian. Conceptual confusion thus serves to make life easier for those who wish to be called Christians but who don't want to be bothered by thinking that much about it. By writing to increase his reader's conceptual clarity, Kierkegaard wants to combat this easy Christianity (what Bonhoeffer called "cheap grace"[18]); he wants to bring to light what is all too easily accepted and ask: But is this truly Christian? As he puts it, "My intention is to make it difficult to become a Christian, yet not more difficult than it is."[19] Conceptual confusion actually robs us of the freedom to become Christians; Kierkegaard, with his ability to establish precise definitions and keep clear on the distinctions crucial to Christian life, is actually making us, as readers, free once again: free to choose the difficult renunciation that is Christian life, where we have to love our neighbor even if he is ugly, morally repellent, or just uninteresting. It is in such a choice that truly Christian action resides.

So how do we move from conceptual confusion to conceptual clarity? Of course, by reading, as already mentioned. However: it is not just any kind of reading that contributes to this transformation. Particular kinds of reading are required, and if we return to Kierkegaard's Preface to *Works of Love*, we find a clue as to *how* we might arrive at conceptual clarity (beyond just knowing *that* this activity, reading, should help).

Thus far we have mainly paid attention to one word from *Works of Love*'s Preface, *deliberation*. Yet the phrase which contains the word *deliberation* also gives a crucial indication as to how a deliberation is to be engaged. Let's return, then, to that first sentence of *Works of Love*:

> These Christian deliberations, which are the fruit of much deliberation, will be understood slowly but then also easily, whereas they will surely become very difficult

18. Bonhoeffer, *Discipleship*, 43–44.
19. *CUP*, 557 / *SKS* 7, 506.

if someone by hasty and curious reading makes them very difficult for himself.[20]

Here Kierkegaard draws a connection between the rate at which one reads and the quality of understanding such a rate produces. When given a book, one might think: the faster I read this, the more quickly I can comprehend its contents and move on to other things. Kierkegaard rejects this commonsense equation. His "deliberations" will be understood, and understood "easily," but only if one reads them "slowly."

Today, throughout the United States of America, there are innumerable classes offered on speed reading (you can do a simple Google search to confirm the fact). These classes promise to give students the ability to read and process information at rates previously unimaginable. Instead of wasting time wrestling with the significance of each word in a sentence, efficient speed readers learn to pick out relevant nouns and verbs, passing over the extraneous jumble of language so that meaning can be grasped quickly and confidently.

Though it promises swift comprehension, according to Kierkegaard this is not the actual end result of speed reading. One may move through a book quickly with such methods, but this does not mean one has understood the material. Paradoxically, the reader who takes the time to sit with one sentence and truly understand it is making a more "efficient" use of her time than a speed reader who glides through an entire book in that same time—for the first reader has at least understood something; the second reader, nothing.

Our culture is obsessed with making the "best" use of one's time, with its seminars on time management and maximization initiatives. Kierkegaard does not necessarily castigate this concern. Only, he holds the fulfillment of the goal to be counterintuitive. It is a better use of one's time to spend more days reading a book, not less. Kierkegaard turns efficiency on its head by asking "What is the purpose of reading? And how might we best get there?"

20. *WL*, 3 / *SKS* 9, 11.

Kierkegaard is an advocate of slow reading. Rather than quickly moving on from a text once you have grasped its general meaning, Kierkegaard believes you should wrestle with words, turning over each phrase, pondering possible examples of the author's meaning, stopping to consider other potential meanings of a text beyond one's initial interpretation.

Perhaps, while reading, you look up a word in your dictionary, making sure you're conscious of all the word's varied nuances. Or a particular sentence makes you think, so you stop, open up your journal, and jot down a few of the ruminations your reading has inspired. Or maybe you really fall in love with an individual passage, so much so that you decide to commit it to memory. There are myriad ways to read slowly.

In a documentary made about his life in 2002,[21] Jacques Derrida—a French philosopher and one of the best readers of the last century—was giving an interviewer a tour of his extensive library when the interviewer asked how many of the books he had read. "Three or four," Derrida replied, "but I've read them very well." That is the kind of reader Kierkegaard thinks you should be.

In the next chapter, I will return to this theme of how speed reading can be counterproductive and even a vice. For now, let's take up an example of how quick versus slow readings can affect the understanding of a text by looking at different interpretations of the book we have been considering all along: Kierkegaard's *Works of Love*.

It is actually fairly easy to misunderstand Kierkegaard's distinction in *Works of Love* between *Elskov* and *Kjerlighed* if one has only hastily and superficially perused the relevant texts. This kind of misunderstanding is evident in published interpretations of *Works of Love*, such as by Knud Ejler Løgstrup, who believes Kierkegaard is asking us to break off all familial and romantic relationships,[22] or by Theodor Adorno, who accused *Works of Love* of abstracting from the neighbor's concrete physical needs.[23]

---

21. Dick and Kofman, dirs., *Derrida*.
22. See Løgstrup, *The Ethical Demand*.
23. See Adorno, "On Kierkegaard's Doctrine of Love."

These are readings that take Kierkegaard's split between *Elskov* and *Kjerlighed* and extrapolate from it, constructing hastily cobbled together critiques without really pausing to consider the specific associations Kierkegaard means to give the differentiation.[24] These are readers who "by hasty and curious reading" make the deliberations "very difficult" for themselves (and the others whom they influence).[25]

A good counterexample to this type of rushed, superficial reading can be found in John J. Davenport's recently published essay, "The Integration of Neighbor-Love and Special Loves in Kierkegaard and von Hildebrand." Through careful attention to a few judicious selections from *Works of Love*, Davenport demonstrates that despite the contrast between *Elskov* and *Kjerlighed*, Kierkegaard does not intend to get rid of *Elskov* in favor of *Kjerlighed*, and thus he does not mean to eliminate all familial, philial, or romantic relations in favor of the neighbor. Although there is a difference between *Elskov* and *Kjerlighed*, the two are not necessarily contrastive in an existential sense; that is to say, *Elskov* and *Kjerlighed* can both be a part of a faithful Christian life.

Davenport suggests the following pattern of integration, which I find persuasive. *Kjerlighed* is the basic reality of every truly Christian life. It applies equally to all—mother, father, stranger, enemy, friend. And it means that each of our relationships should be, at their most fundamental level, about helping the other person love God more fully; every relationship should be missional. At the same time, this basic reality of *Kjerlighed*—which applies equally to all—does not rule out the legitimacy of special relationships with people to whom we are naturally drawn, by familial inheritance or any other affinity. Instead, Kierkegaard holds that special relationships should be welcomed and celebrated, while at the same time being checked and governed by *Kjerlighed*. We

---

24. See, e.g., my critique of Adorno and Løgstrup in "Concrete *and* Otherworldly." Adorno is paradigmatic here over Løgstrup, in that he has a prefabricated critique of nineteenth-century bourgeois ideology that he then applies to Kierkegaard. See also Adorno's *Kierkegaard*.

25. *WL*, 3 / *SKS* 9, 11.

can enjoy friendship, delighting in the presence of the other, while at the same time obeying *Kjerlighed*'s imperative not to make the other part of my project of self-assertion, always having her individuality and God-relationship in mind.[26]

Davenport labels this integration of *Elskov* and *Kjerlighed* the "agapic infusion"[27] of special relationships, and he provides an example in the character of Cordelia, who in Shakespeare's *King Lear* loves her father but refuses to flatter him as her sisters do. Cordelia treats her father as her father and as a human being, as someone who has a special relationship with her but who also is his own person with his own salvation to work out in fear and trembling. By the pattern of love embodied in her actions, we are thus able to see that Cordelia is both daughter and Christian, whereas her sisters are certainly daughters, but may not be Christians—at least not in the moments recorded in the drama's text.[28]

It is evident that Davenport's interpretation is the result of slow reading and extended deliberation. He pays attention to all relevant texts, rather than hastily choosing those that fit the argument he wants to make. He makes precise, considered judgments that reference direct textual evidence. He thinks of examples that illustrate Kierkegaard's meaning. So why is this important? Does it just mean that Davenport is a slightly better scholar than Løgstrup or Adorno?

Recall the earlier discussion of the importance of the distinction between *Elskov* and *Kjerlighed*. If Christian life depends on conceptual clarity, and becoming clear about concepts depends on slow reading, then slow reading is essential to Christian life. It is not just a matter of becoming a slightly better scholar. It is a matter of what sort of life you are going to live.

26. Davenport, "The Integration of Neighbor-Love and Special Loves," 57–63.

27. Ibid., 49.

28. Ibid., 60.

4 Appropriation

"APPROPRIATION": TO TAKE SOMETHING outside the self and make it one's own. We do this all the time with food, by ingesting it and literally making it a part of our bodies. But we also do it with texts. Eugene Peterson, translator of *The Message*, once wrote a plea for this type of appropriative reading titled *Eat This Book* (alluding to how the prophet Ezekiel was once commanded to devour a scroll), and there are parallels between reading and eating: in both we are taking what is outside the self and spending time with it, working on it, to make it our own. Further, reading and eating are both activities that affect the way we live our lives, hopefully providing nourishment and causing growth.

Appropriation is a major theme in Kierkegaard's writings.[1] I will take a moment to describe what he means by it in a broader sense before turning to its more local importance in his philosophy of reading.

Kierkegaard's most famous journal entry is about appropriation. If you are looking for one place to locate the birth of existentialist philosophy, you could do worse than the following lines:

> What I really need is to get clear about *what I am to do*, not what I must know, except insofar as knowledge must precede every act. What matters is to find my purpose,

---

1. In Danish, the word is *Tilegnelse*. For a concise summary of Kierkegaard's usage, see Sean Anthony Turchin, "Appropriation."

to see what it really is that God wills that *I* shall do; the crucial thing is to find a truth that is truth *for me*, to find *the idea for which I am willing to live and die*. Of what use would it be to me to discover a so-called objective truth, to work through the philosophical systems so that I could, if asked, make critical judgments about them, could point out the fallacies in each system; of what use would it be to me to be able to develop a theory of the state, getting details from various sources and combining them into a whole, and constructing a world I did not live in but merely held up for others to see; of what use would it be to me to be able to formulate the meaning of Christianity, to be able to explain many specific points— if it had no deeper meaning *for me and for my life*?[2]

Understanding this passage requires an extra measure of care. It is easy to think Kierkegaard is saying: some things are true for me, some things are true for you, and what's important is that you find *your* truth. This sort of view is usually summarized with the phrase "all truth is relative," meaning that there is no one truth, no objective truth, but simply a variety of perspectival opinions. But that is not what Kierkegaard is saying.

Kierkegaard means to say that, of all the truth that is objectively out there, he wants to find the kind of truth that he can make his own, a truth that will cause a change in the way he lives his life. He wants not only to learn but to grow, in an existential sense: to become a single individual, someone who does not simply rely on what others tell him, but is passionately committed to the encounter with truth that he himself has had, apart from all others.

The context for the passage is important. Kierkegaard wrote these words just before he began his Master's work, when he was trying to figure out what field he should enter. He eventually chose philosophy, but this doesn't mean Kierkegaard thinks philosophy is the "correct" field. It was the correct field *for him*. The important question is: what is the field within which I could spend my entire life pursuing its truths and never weary? And how would

2. Here I use the Hongs' translation of *Pap*. I A 75, Gilleleje, August 1, 1835, in *JP* 5100; cf. *KJN* 1, 19 / *SKS* 17, 24.

these truths affect my life—what shape would they give it, if I really appropriate what I discover? These are questions of personal inclination that cannot be answered by Kierkegaard. Instead of an answer, here Kierkegaard points us to the right question: is this the truth *for me*?

Another way to put this is that Kierkegaard does not undermine the objective character of truth, but emphasizes the importance of its subjective appropriation. In *Concluding Unscientific Postscript*, published about thirteen years after the "Gilleleje" journal entry referenced above, Kierkegaard develops this emphasis on appropriation at length via his concept of "subjectivity." He explains the concept of subjectivity by reflecting on what it means for an individual to have faith.

Christian faith involves an objective knowledge-claim: at a certain point in history, God became an individual human being.[3] This claim, though objective, cannot be known with certainty. We were not there in first-century Palestine; and even if we were, Christ's divinity is cloaked by his indistinguishable humanity (what Kierkegaard calls his "incognito"). To have faith is to hold with subjective passion that an objective uncertainty is the truth. Thus, one takes what is an uncertain truth and bases the rest of one's life upon this "fact": this is what appropriation looks like when dealing with matters of faith. "[T]ruth," as Kierkegaard puts it, "is the self-activity of appropriation";[4] it is taking a truth outside the self and making it truth *for me*, the basis of how I conceive my self-identity and the guide for all decisions I come to make.

For the Christian, appropriation means relating to the incarnation of God in Jesus Christ with an infinite passion, even if such a fact is uncertain:

> *An objective uncertainty, held fast through appropriation with the most passionate inwardness, is the truth,* the

---

3. I would be remiss not to point out a fundamental theological error of Kierkegaard here. It absolutely should not be glossed over that God became incarnate in a Jewish human being. See especially Jennings, *The Christian Imagination*, chapter 6, "Those Near Belonging," 250–88.

4. *CUP*, 242 / *SKS* 7, 220.

highest truth there is for an *existing* person . . . Objectively he then has only uncertainty, but this is precisely what intensifies the infinite passion of inwardness, and truth is precisely the daring venture of choosing the objective uncertainty with the passion of the infinite.[5]

The thought of God, and the person of Jesus Christ—whom we read about in the Gospels—is appropriated this way. The person of faith has an absolute dedication to what remains absolutely uncertain. Other truths have different modes of appropriation, their own modes which are appropriate to them, as we will see later in this chapter when I outline a Kierkegaardian approach to scientific literature.

But first I hope to further clarify the task of appropriation by citing two counterexamples Kierkegaard develops. The first counterexample, speculative philosophy, can be found in *Concluding Unscientific Postscript*; the second, the difference between admiration and imitation, is in the later book *Practice in Christianity*.

(1) What Kierkegaard calls "speculative philosophy" was the creation of a brilliant generation of German Idealist thinkers, including Immanuel Kant, J. G. Fichte, and F. W. J. Schelling.[6] The apotheosis of German idealist thought can be found in the philosophy of G. W. F. Hegel, who had a major influence on the Danish philosophers popular in Kierkegaard's age.[7] Hegel's special invention was a sophisticated dialectical method that aimed to produce truth as the result of a whole and evolving structure; rather than any one of his individual sentences being true, each corrected the other until the end product of actually manifest truth eventually appeared.[8] Like the other speculative philosophers, Hegel hoped

---

5. *CUP*, 203 / *SKS* 7, 186.

6. The literature on German Idealism is vast. See especially Ameriks, ed., *The Cambridge Companion to German Idealism*, and Schindler, *The Perfection of Freedom*.

7. For an extensive history, see Jon Stewart, *A History of Hegelianism in Golden Age Denmark*, Tomes I and II.

8. I have found Yirmayahu Yovel's translation of and commentary on Hegel's "Preface" to the *Phenomenology of Spirit* to be an immensely helpful introduction to his philosophy.

his philosophy would be a true mirror (in Latin, *speculum*) to the world, comprehending its essence in the medium of thought.

What Kierkegaard rejects in this approach is precisely its emphasis on comprehension as the goal of thought (rather than, say, the purpose of thought being to serve as a goad to obedient action). True speculation is the goal of speculative philosophy, but this should never be the goal of actually existing human beings, who exist in the flux of time and are constantly compelled to make decisions that are by no means based on complete comprehension of the matter at hand.[9] To be an existing person means to risk making decisions, even ultimate decisions, with incomplete information. The goal of knowledge cannot be comprehension (because we never arrive at it, thus creating an insoluble contradiction if we in fact take this as our goal), and not only *cannot* comprehension be the goal of knowledge, it *should* not be. To want complete comprehension is to be mistaken about what it means to be a human being. It is to take an activity like reading and make it into an end-in-itself, rather than the means to furthering one's love of God.

To say that comprehension not only cannot but should not be the goal of knowledge usefully leads us into the realm of what is called "theological anthropology," which speaks to what it means to be a human person given our creation in God's image. A brief look at Kierkegaard's theological anthropology will give us some insight into the fundamental truths that structure his philosophy of reading.

Basic to Kierkegaard's anthropology is that we are not just spirits but embodied, temporal beings.[10] We exist in the flux of time. God placed us in a world of becoming, where any pretension to comprehension is illusory, because that which was to be comprehended has already changed.[11] This lack of comprehensive abil-

---

9. See *CUP*, 209 / *SKS* 7, 192, on "objective uncertainty" and "ignorance."

10. See especially Kierkegaard's 1847 text *The Sickness unto Death*, now with helpful commentary by Sponheim, *Existing before God*. Cf. Kierkegaard's *The Concept of Anxiety* with my commentary "Classical Greek Sculpture in *The Concept of Anxiety*." Cf. also Marrs, "To Become Transfigured."

11. See especially *CUP*, 81 / *SKS* 7, 80–81.

ity is not to be mourned; it should point us to what we were made to be, not objective comprehenders but subjective passionate risk takers who have faith—or trust—that their action is based on truth as it has been revealed.[12] It is right and good that human beings are existing, limited, passionate, gambling creatures; that is what they were made to be. And Kierkegaard's philosophy of reading reflects this. We should not read for comprehension (illusory at any rate), but use words as a goad to action. Why we read should reflect who we are as human beings.

Speculative philosophy reflects a mistaken theological anthropology, as if human beings were eternal comprehending machines, minds-on-a-stick who can perceive essences but take no action and make no risks. Kierkegaard's existential philosophy returns the accent on appropriation to its proper place.[13] We perceive some fragment of truth and act accordingly, threading it into our limited and fluctuating world as our stand of faith, our risky wager, that this is the truth and I am living for it.

(2) We have covered Kierkegaard's theory of subjectivity, noted the place of appropriation within it, summarized his critique of objectivity and speculative philosophy, and registered how the positions Kierkegaard takes are grounded in his theological anthropology. This is all good and necessary work. But what does the neglect of appropriation look like on the ground, in a concrete sense?

Kierkegaard provides a vivid example in his book *For Self-Examination*, though it must be admitted that he cribs the example from a Hebrew text that is at least as vivid. Kierkegaard recounts the story of Nathan and David to illustrate the importance of appropriation. This story is originally told in 2 Samuel 12. The context

12. See ibid., 204 / 187: "Without risk, no faith. Faith is the contradiction between the infinite passion of inwardness and the objective uncertainty. If I am able to apprehend God objectively, I do not have faith; but because I cannot do this, I must have faith. If I want to keep myself in faith, I must continually see to it that in the objective uncertainty I am 'out on 70,000 fathoms of water' and still have faith."

13. I say "return" because, in antiquity, the accent was in fact on appropriation. See Hadot, *Philosophy as a Way of Life*.

for the story is the infamous narrative of David and Bathsheba, in which the king supposedly after God's own heart (1 Samuel 13:14) sees a woman bathing, has his men abduct her, has sex with her (or, more accurately put, rapes her), then has her husband killed to get him out of the way. After all this, David appears not the least bit remorseful; he is a powerful man and has acted in accordance with his power. Then Nathan, a prophet, pays him a visit:

> And the Lord sent Nathan to David, and he came to him and said to him: "Two men there were in a single town, one was rich and the other poor. The rich man had sheep and cattle, in great abundance. And the poor man had nothing save one little ewe that he had bought. And he nurtured her and raised her with his sons. From his crust she would eat and from his cup she would drink and in his lap she would lie, and she was to him like a daughter. And a wayfarer came to the rich man, and it seemed a pity to him to take from his own sheep and cattle to prepare for the traveler who had come to him, and he took the poor man's ewe and prepared it for the man who had come to him."[14]

The story sucks David in—he is absorbed, then angry, and he promises to execute righteous judgment upon the perpetrator. It is at this point that Nathan turns to him and exclaims, "You are the man!" Broken by the power of story, David finally understands what he has done. He dons sackcloth and weeps, speaking these words (Ps 51:1–3):

> Have mercy on me, O God,
>> according to your steadfast love;
> According to your abundant mercy
>> blot out my transgressions.
> Wash me thoroughly from my iniquity,
>> and cleanse me from my sin.
> For I know my transgressions,
>> and my sin is ever before me.

---

14. 2 Samuel 12:1–4, Alter's translation (*The Prophets*, 351–52).

In his recounting of this extraordinary narrative, Kierkegaard zeroes in on one moment in particular: the instant when David shifts from understanding Nathan's story to be about another person to being about himself ("my sin is ever before me"). In *For Self-Examination*, Kierkegaard provides his readers a kind of midrash on this moment:

> See, the tale the prophet told was a story, but this "Thou art the man"—this was another story—this was the transition to the subjective.
>
> But do you not believe that David himself was well aware beforehand how abominable it is to have a woman's husband killed in order to marry her? Do you not believe that David, the great poet, could easily describe this (eloquently, terrifyingly, shockingly)? Then, too, do you not believe that David was well aware that he was guilty and what he was guilty of? And yet, yet, yet someone from the outside was needed, someone who said to him: You.[15]

This turn from the objective to the subjective is precisely the moment of appropriation. What the biblical text of 2 Samuel gives us is thus an act of appropriation happening in real time, so that we might be able to see what this concept looks like and what types of consequences might result from its practice. For David—as for most of us—it looks like repentance.

Kierkegaard makes a further point beyond the text, adding his own philosophical spin on the Nathan-David story. He writes that it is necessary "[w]hen you read God's Word, in everything you read, continually to say to yourself: It is I to whom it is speaking, it is I about whom it is speaking—this is earnestness, precisely this is earnestness."[16] In other words, the significance of the point Nathan makes to David is applicable not only to David; it provides a kind of rubric for reading in general. Nathan's exclamation to David is applicable universally to every reader of the Scriptures. Each passage, every last one, addresses us and says, "You are the man!" If we fail to appropriate the meaning of the text, missing

15. *FSE*, 38–39 / *SKS* 13, 65.
16. Ibid., 36 / 63.

how the words apply *to me*, address *me*, and tell *me* to change, we remain in the position David was before Nathan visited him: separated from the truth, alienated from God and from who we really are. The words of Scripture are there in order to change our lives, to be appropriated and seen in their uniquely personal resonance, for you and you alone. You are the man!

The contrast between different ways of approaching knowledge that we have been drawing here—between subjective and objective, existential and speculative—maps directly on to different ways of reading. We can at this point further elucidate the contrast Kierkegaard is drawing with reference to Augustine's juxtaposition of two different "appetites" for knowledge, *curiositas* and *studiositas*, the subject of a recent thought-provoking book by Paul J. Griffiths.

Believe it or not, for Augustine curiosity (*curiositas*, in Latin) was a vice. Drawing primarily on Book 10 of Augustine's treatise *On the Trinity*, Griffiths explicates the concept of *curiositas* as follows:

> Curiosity is a particular appetite, which is to say a particular ordering of the affections, or, more succinctly, a particular intentional love. Its object, what it wants, is new knowledge, a previously unexperienced reflexive intimacy with some creature. And what it seeks to do with that knowledge is control, dominate, or make a private possession of it. Curiosity is, then, in brief, *appetite for the ownership of new knowledge*[.][17]

You may have noticed that Kierkegaard uses "curiosity" in a similar way in the Preface to *Works of Love*, which we studied in detail in the previous chapter.[18] Curiosity thus refers to a kind of relentless desire for new knowledge, which when achieved results in the

---

17. Griffiths, *Intellectual Appetite*, 20; italics original.

18. *WL*, 3 / *SKS* 9, 11: "These Christian deliberations, which are the fruit of much deliberation, will be understood slowly but then also easily, whereas they will surely become very difficult if someone by hasty and curious reading makes them very difficult for himself." Haste and the search for new knowledge are tandem impulses, as I argue below.

newly minted knower being able to wield her knowledge as a possession (something under her control).

For the vice of *curiositas*, there is a corresponding and corrective virtue: *studiositas*. Again, it is helpful to turn to Griffiths's summary, which synthesizes several Augustinian texts:

> Studiousness, like curiosity, is a particular love, a specific ordering of the affections. And like curiosity it has knowledge as its object, which it seeks. But the studious do not seek to sequester, own, possess, or dominate what they hope to know; they want, instead, to participate lovingly in it, to respond to it knowingly as gift rather than as potential possession, to treat it as icon rather than as spectacle. A preliminary definition of studiousness, then, is: *appetite for closer reflexive intimacy with the gift.*[19]

As Griffith's text develops from these initial definitions, it becomes clear that the key word being used is *intimacy*.[20] Notice, however, that "intimacy" is used in both definitions. The difference between *curiositas* and *studiositas* has to do with the kind of intimacy each achieves. *Curiositas* is characterized by superficial intimacy; one knows just enough of the object to assert control over it. To transcode this into the terms of reading: one has skimmed just enough of the text to write an essay. *Studiositas*, on the other hand, is characterized by deep intimacy; one never stops pursuing further knowledge of the subject at hand and is aware that one can never control that which is essentially inexhaustible. *Studiositas* is driven by love and an ever-increasing sense of delight, rather than the desire to dominate. Instead of changing the text and using it to further her own pursuits, the reader who embodies *studiositas* is changed by the text. As she is led deeper into the text's mysteries, spending more and more time with this object which causes profound, lasting joy, she appropriates the text as it works its way into her life, giving her actions and her self-identity a particular direction—that direction which is always potentially within a text

---

19. Griffiths, *Intellectual Appetite*, 21; italics original.

20. See in particular ibid., 118–19.

and can only be activated by the dedicated reader. *Studiositas* thus summarizes the type of reading that produces appropriation.

In *Practice in Christianity* (1850), published one year before *For Self-Examination*, Kierkegaard gives us a positive concrete example of what he thinks the practice of appropriation looks like. The example is found in the person of Jesus Christ, particularly when Christ is before Pilate. Kierkegaard gives a playful exegesis of John 18:33–38, filling in a silence in a way that the rabbis of the Talmud would likely have admired:[21]

> For what is truth, and in what sense was Christ the truth? The first question, as is well known, was asked by Pilate, and another question is whether he really cared to have his question answered; in any case, in one sense his question was altogether appropriate, and in another sense it was as inappropriate as possible. Pilate asks Christ the question: What is truth? But Christ was indeed the truth; therefore the question was entirely appropriate. Yes, and yet in another sense, no. That it can occur to Pilate at that moment to question Christ in this way demonstrates precisely that he has no eye at all for truth. Christ's life was in fact the truth, and therefore Christ himself says ... For this I was born, and for this I have come into the world, that I shall witness to the truth.[22]
>
> . . .
>
> Thus Christ is the truth in the sense that to *be* the truth is the only true explanation of what truth is. Therefore one can ask an apostle, one can ask a Christian, "What is truth?" and in answer to the question the apostle and this Christian will point to Christ and say: Look at him, learn from him, he was the truth. This means that truth in the sense in which Christ is the truth is not a sum of statements, not a definition etc., but a life.[23]

---

21. For a judicious selection, see Bokser and Bokser, eds., *The Talmud.*

22. *PC*, 203 / *SKS* 12, 200.

23. Ibid., 205 / 201–2.

When Pilate asks Jesus "What is truth?" (John 18:38), Jesus responds with silence. Why? Because the answer is already right there in front of him, though not present in words.

Truth is a person, truth is a life: there is no truth without appropriation. Without appropriation, what would be true remains an abstraction: a theoretical statement. Truth requires what Kierkegaard calls a "redoubling," a putting into action of the ideas found in texts.[24] It is only there, within the existential realm, that action enables the real existence of truth. We are not just thinking things, and thus "truth" that has not entered the realm of action remains only a questionable hypothesis. A theoretical statement may or may not be true—we won't know until it is lived. That is why speculation and abstract thought is of little value if it lacks its counterpart of appropriation.

Christ shows us what it means to synthesize thought and action. The relevant text in the background of John 18 is Isaiah 53:4–7:

> Indeed, he has borne our illness,
>   and our sorrows he has carried.
> But we had reckoned him plagued,
>   God-stricken and tormented.
> Yet he was wounded for our crimes,
>   crushed for our transgressions.
> The chastisement that restored our well-being he bore,
>   and through his bruising we were healed.
> All of us strayed like sheep,
>   each turned to his own way,
> and the Lord brought down upon him
>   the crimes of all of us.
> Afflicted and tormented,
>   he opened not his mouth.
> Like a lamb led to the slaughter

24. Cf. 2 Timothy 3:16–17: "All scripture is inspired by God and is useful for teaching, for reproof, for correction, and for training in righteousness, so that everyone who belongs to God may be proficient, equipped for every good work." According to this Scripture on the purpose of Scripture, it is evident that the purpose of the scriptural text is to enable the reader-hearer to be equipped for action.

> and like an ewe before her shearers
> he opened not his mouth.[25]

Jesus has read this Scripture about a suffering servant standing silent before his accusers, and he has put the text into practice. He *is* the suffering servant; redemption of sin is borne in him, through his person, in his existence. In Jesus, Isaiah 53 is no longer a hypothetical text about what it would take to redeem the erring peoples of the earth. It has a physical meaning in Jesus' life; his person is the meaning of the text, because he has appropriated it and given manifestation to the truth of the text *via* his own dynamic life. The same could be said about an earlier passage from Luke 4, where Jesus stands in the Nazareth synagogue and reads from Isaiah about good news being proclaimed to the poor, release being given to captives, sight being restored to the blind, and freedom being given to the oppressed. After reading, he simply stands before them, shows his person to their watchful eyes, and says: "Today this scripture has been fulfilled in your hearing" (Luke 4:21b). Fulfilled how? In his very person! He himself is the embodiment of the promises come to pass.

So, we have defined appropriation as the subjective self-activation of truth within a given person's life, and we have seen concrete examples of how this either happens (Jesus) or fails to happen (David [that is, before Nathan forces the subjective turn on him]). What remains to be developed is *how* we go about cultivating appropriation as an element of our reading practice, and seeing what this looks like for those of us who are not Jesus.

Kierkegaard gives his audience guidance as to how appropriation can occur through reading in his Preface to *Upbuilding Discourses in Various Spirits* (1847):

> Although this little book (it can be called an occasional discourse, yet without having the occasion that makes the speaker and makes him an *authority* or the occasion that makes the reader and makes him a *learner*) in the situation of *actuality* is like a fancy, a dream in the daytime, yet it is not without confidence and not without hope of

25. Alter's translation (*The Prophets*, 802).

fulfillment. It seeks that single individual, to whom it gives itself wholly, by whom it wishes to be received as if it had arisen in his own heart, that single individual whom I with joy and gratitude call *my* reader, that single individual, who willingly reads slowly, reads repeatedly, and who reads aloud—for his own sake. If it finds him, then in the remoteness of separation the understanding is complete when he keeps the book and the understanding to himself in the inwardness of appropriation.[26]

In these rich sentences, we have confirmation of the point argued thus far in the current chapter: appropriation is an essential element of Kierkegaard's philosophy of reading, such that an "understanding" of the text fails to be "complete" unless the reader "keeps the book and the understanding to himself in the inwardness of appropriation."[27] Beyond such confirmation, we also have Kierkegaard's word on how a reader might practice a reading oriented toward appropriation. According to this passage, Kierkegaard's ideal reader is one "who willingly reads slowly, reads repeatedly, and who reads aloud."[28]

We have come across one of these directives before, in the Preface to *Works of Love* where Kierkegaard states that only someone who reads slowly will readily understand the text. There are two additional reading practices listed in the *Upbuilding Discourses in Various Spirits* Preface. The ideal reader not only "reads slowly"; she "reads repeatedly" and she "reads aloud." Let's take these last two practices one at a time.

Recall the earlier distinction between *curiositas* and *studiositas*. As Kierkegaard indicates in the *Works of Love* Preface, the curious reader reads "hastily."[29] This means not only that she reads at a fairly rapid pace; it also implies that she is much less likely to read a text more than once. Remember, the goal of the curious reader is

---

26. *UDVS*, 5 / *SKS* 8, 121.

27. Ibid.; "in the inwardness of appropriation (*i Tilegnelsens Inderlighed*)."

28. Ibid.; "reads slowly, reads repeatedly, and. . . reads aloud (*læser langsomt, læser gjentagent, og. . . læser høit*)."

29. *WL*, 3 / *SKS* 9, 11.

APPROPRIATION

simply to get enough of a handle on a text in order to use it for her own purposes. The studious reader, on the other hand, has every reason to read a text multiple times. She wants deep intimacy, and repetition is a vehicle to this goal.

How so? When we first encounter an idea, we may be simply curious about it: "Here is a new thing. What does it mean?" Repeated encounters enable a different sort of relation: "Here is a truth, but how is it truth *for me*?" Repetition enables intimacy at an existential level. One is no longer reading to discover the new, but to enter more deeply into a text one already loves, and in doing so one should—according to Kierkegaard—ask oneself if one's life corresponds to one's love. "Is this text, which I have found both to be true and to be true for me, simply an abstract idea, or has it had the kind of impact where I could say that I have been faithful, in my own personal existence, to what I have discovered there?" Repeated readings give one the chance to repeatedly ask this question, and to each time take a small step closer to a full appropriation, a complete translation of the truth of the text into the daily patterns of one's life. So then, "read repeatedly."

What does reading aloud have to do with appropriation? Why would it make a difference whether you lend your voice to a text or silently process it in your mind? Beyond the terse imperative in the Preface to *Upbuilding Discourses in Various Spirits* ("read aloud"), Kierkegaard gives us a further clue to the purpose of vocal reading in the Preface to *For Self-Examination*:

> My dear reader, read aloud, if possible! If you do so, allow me to thank you for it; if you not only do it yourself, if you also influence others to do it, allow me to thank each one of them, and you again and again! By reading aloud you will gain the strongest impression that you have only yourself to consider, not me, who, after all, am "without authority," nor others, which would be a distraction.[30]

There is no way to prove this with certainty, but I believe Kierkegaard is making a kind of phenomenological point here. When you

30. *FSE*, 3 / *SKS* 13, 33.

read aloud, you simply experience the text addressing you—you in particular—to a greater extent than you would reading silently. It is as if someone were standing right before you, addressing these words to you and pressing to see if you have been faithful to the truth that is in them. Except it is just you, you alone with the words, so that the address they speak doesn't go anywhere; it doesn't leave the room to visit anyone else; it doesn't flit away before you can really grasp its meaning; the text pins you down and places you in question. The address remains, but it speaks as forcefully as a Socrates (or a Nathan), if you read aloud. Ultimately, on account of the non-universality of perceptual experiences, there is no way for me to confirm that this method will work for you in this way. All I can say is: try it. See if it makes an impression.

So then, read slowly: take the time necessary to really grasp the concepts at play. Read repeatedly: commit to entering more deeply into familiar ideas, rather than constantly seeking the new. And read aloud: let the text speak an address to you, so that you know—like Matthew in Caravaggio's extraordinary painting *The Calling of St. Matthew*—that it is you who are being called out, you who are being asked if your life has changed in accord with the truth you have encountered. These three practices together constitute the method whereby the Kierkegaardian reader "inwardly appropriates" what she finds on the page.[31] It is *how* the reader makes truth her own and lives it out, just as Christ stood before the Nazareth synagogue and before Pilate, proclaiming: "I *am* the truth. The truth is my existence."

There is perhaps a certain unapproachability in what has been developed so far. The example used, Christ, is an extreme one; it is the highest pinnacle a human being can reach with respect to the appropriation of truth and its identification with one's life. Not every example of appropriation need be so extreme. In what remains of this chapter, I hope to show that appropriation can happen even in perfectly ordinary moments of reading life: namely, in the reading of scientific texts.

---

31. Cf. *UDVS*, 5 / *SKS* 8, 121.

Recall that expansiveness is one of the virtues of Kierkegaard's philosophy of reading, in comparison to Augustine. By briefly looking at scientific research and placing it in dialogue with the Psalms, we can see just how wide the net of upbuilding literature can be.

Scientific literature should not be completely divorced from upbuilding literature, as if the two remain necessarily unrelated. On the contrary, it seems to me that being a scientific naturalist makes you a better reader of the Psalms. Take E. O. Wilson, for example. This is a man who has dedicated his life to the love of ants. He began collecting specimens at the age of nine and knew that he wanted to be an entomologist at age eighteen.[32] Wilson has done in-depth studies not only of the anatomy of ants, but also of the chemical compounds that make up their communication patterns *via* pheromones, and—building off this work—the more general social patterns and behaviors of ants.[33] Now, what do you think such a man has in mind when he reads in Psalm 148:10 that God has made "creeping things" upon the earth that praise God? Much more than I have in my mind when I read the verse, I freely admit. Wilson would be able to connect the phrase "creeping things" to the intricate designs of ant anatomy, with their six jointed legs attached to a thorax, resting just beneath their eminently useful antennae; he would be able to think of Dufour's gland and its central role in communication of the trail pheromones so essential to an ant mound's discovery of food;[34] in short, Wilson would have all his knowledge of ants in mind when he envisions the creeping things God has made as they praise their God. I do not have such extensive knowledge of ants, and I am a worse reader of this Psalm for it. Wilson has many more opportunities than I to praise God when reading this Psalm, all of which unfold from that one phrase, "creeping things." The wonder of the intricacy of God's creation leads to praise, but one can only be so led *if* one is aware of the

32. Wilson recounts the story of his life in his autobiographical *Naturalist*.

33. See, for example, Wilson, "Enemy Specification"; *Naturalist*, chapter 15, "Ants," 282–306; Wilson and Hölldobler, *The Ants*.

34. Wilson actually discovered this role. See *Naturalist*, 290.

intricacy at hand. One cannot wonder at intricacy if one is not aware of intricacy. This is what scientific study enables.

Correlatively, this does mean that the Psalms have a very important role to play: they activate the potential for praise that is present in the close study of nature. The result of the interplay of science and the Psalms is a virtuous circle, with science providing detailed knowledge that enhances the words of Scripture and Scripture articulating the praise that places scientific detail in its proper creaturely context. Notice that this virtuous circle does not only improve our reading of the Psalms; properly grasped, it also affects how even the most technical scientific paper is read, for the context of praise can enhance any detail. Just like novels, then, the pages of a scientific journal can be, in Kierkegaard's words, "a place of prayer."[35]

This sort of experience can be repeated across many Psalms, and all the domains of science are potentially found therein. If all truth is God's truth, then all truths can be upbuilding. Within Jewish and Christian Scripture, the Psalms preeminently demonstrate the cosmic scope of the good worshipper's interests. You don't need to give up on your reading being upbuilding if you go into the sciences. These fields of inquiry, just like any other, can be approached in such a way that they increase your love of God.

---

35. *LR*, 21 / *SKS* 8, 23.

5 Don't Read, Act!

KIERKEGAARD HAD A LOVE for paradoxes. In fact, he writes in *Philosophical Fragments* that "the thinker without the paradox is like a lover without passion: a mediocre fellow."[1] The final chapter of this book celebrates just one of Kierkegaard's many beloved paradoxes: namely, that some of Kierkegaard's most profound comments on reading bid the reader to stop reading.

Certainly, the situation is a paradoxical one. Yet it does not indicate that Kierkegaard is simply a contradictory thinker, filled with the irreconcilable thoughts typical of a writer who fails to make his material cohere. Kierkegaard's imperative for the reader to stop her reading is rather born directly from his philosophy of reading, which recognizes that reading has a proper end.[2] The goal of reading is for it to end in action, and for that action to be undertaken in obedience to God.

In other words, even though Kierkegaard clearly has a high view of what reading can do, and even though he did spend much of his own life reading, he does not believe reading should be an end in itself. Its purpose should be making clear how one must act. Reading is a reflective activity that should always be oriented toward returning us to our individual existence with renewed

---

1. *PF*, 37 / *SKS* 4, 242–43.

2. Throughout this chapter, I mean the word *end* in its dual sense, as both cessation and goal.

purpose; it should fill our sails again with a favorable wind to take us in the direction God is asking us to go. Reading, even some forms of studious reading, can easily become a vice if its purpose is forgotten. So: Kierkegaard—a great reader himself and the author of a highly useful philosophy of reading—paradoxically has this final message for us: don't read, act![3]

There are (at least) two different locations where Kierkegaard writes directly about this topic; I will briefly mention one and focus more extensively on the other. Kierkegaard speaks with great acuity about the dangers of speculative philosophy and its objective disinterest in actual existence (actual existence: that is, the concrete, daily living of a life) in his work *Concluding Unscientific Postscript*. The book's topic is speculative philosophy, with Kierkegaard arguing that it is a mode of thinking that would prefer to read about and observe the world rather than act within it. The argument in *Concluding Unscientific Postscript*—lengthy though it may be—is fully worth the reader's time and energy to work through. However, it remains the case that Kierkegaard speaks most movingly about the necessary shift from reading to action in another of his books, *For Self-Examination* (1851).

In *For Self-Examination*, Kierkegaard offers an extended reflection on James 1:22–23, which begins with the following two sentences: "But be doers of the Word, and not only hearers of it, whereby you deceive yourselves. If anyone is a hearer of the Word and not a doer of it, he is like a man who observes his bodily face in a mirror, for he would observe himself and go away and at once forget what he was like."[4] Like Luther, Kierkegaard appreciates the costly faith these verses require, speaking to the necessity of active response as a consequence of any true hearing of the Word.[5]

3. See Pattison, *Kierkegaard, Religion and the Nineteenth-Century*, 223, 234–35.

4. Translation of James 1:22–23 taken from *FSE*, 13 / *SKS* 13, 43.

5. Luther speaks to the necessity of responsive works in one of his most well-known texts, *The Freedom of a Christian*. For Luther's appreciation of James, see *Sermons*, Vol. 5, 71–73, from the text *Evangellum von den zehn Aussätzigen*. (That Luther disliked James is a stereotype. In fact, he took many different positions on James, some quite positive.)

In order to further draw out the meaning of these verses, Kierkegaard employs two central metaphors for Scripture: (1) the mirror, and (2) the love letter.

(1) James's epistle states that a person who reads God's Word is "like" someone who "observes his bodily face in a mirror." In *For Self-Examination*, Kierkegaard takes this simile one step further, in a literal direction, and simply states that "God's Word is the mirror."[6]

To understand the equation Kierkegaard is making, and its purpose, it will be helpful for you to imagine you are in front of a mirror. So: you've just gotten up after a long night, full of conversation and inebriation. The first thing you do when you wake up is drag yourself to the bathroom and splash cold water on your face. Then you look up, into a mirror.

What is the purpose of this last act? In desperate circumstances, after a particularly long night, it may be to confirm to yourself that you are still alive and able to move. But generally, the purpose of looking up into a mirror is evaluation. You look in order to scrutinize your appearance. (Are the bags under my eyes that deep? Will people notice?)

In *For Self-Examination*, Kierkegaard assumes that you will agree that self-evaluation is the purpose of the mirror, and constitutes its proper function. This does not mean, however, that the mirror is always used in accordance with its true purpose. Kierkegaard mentions one specific alternative possibility: that one spends one's time observing the mirror itself, rather than using the mirror for self-inspection.

Imagine again those desperate circumstances above mentioned. Add to them an act one is ashamed of, some guilt-ridden folly of the night, perhaps an ill-advised tryst or a few words said in anger. Now imagine dragging yourself to the bathroom the next morning. You splash water on your face—and then what? Maybe you look at yourself, or maybe you instinctively avoid the sight of your own image. For some reason, seeing one's own face would be equivalent to confronting the reality of one's actions. So instead of

6. *FSE*, 25 / *SKS* 13, 53.

looking directly at yourself, eye to eye, you avert your gaze: you inspect the framing of the mirror, you notice a few smudges and flicks of toothpaste and realize that this object needs cleaning; perhaps if you have a background in carpentry or glassmaking you investigate how the mirror was physically constructed, seeing where the seams of human or machine labor remain visible. You do everything, that is, except use the mirror for its true purpose.

For Kierkegaard, this is exactly what many of us do when inspecting the mirror that is God's Word. We avoid contact with ourselves. When asking the question: "What is required in order to look at oneself with true blessing in the mirror of the Word?" Kierkegaard answers "The first requirement is that you must not look at the mirror, observe the mirror, but must see yourself in the mirror."[7]

Just as in our bathroom after a night of partying, there are truths about ourselves in God's Word—which "is indeed the mirror"[8]—that we do not want to confront. From the mirror, we avert our gaze; or, staring and staring *at* the mirror, we dream of things other than ourselves. What does the analogous act look like in relation to Scripture? Basically, according to Kierkegaard, it looks like the vast modern accoutrement to the reading of Scripture usually known as "critical scholarship":

> "God's Word" is indeed the mirror—but, but—oh, how enormously complicated—strictly speaking, how much belongs to "God's Word"? Which books are authentic? Are they really by the apostles, and are the apostles really trustworthy? Have they personally seen everything, or have they perhaps only heard about various things from others? As for ways of reading, there are thirty thousand different ways. And then this crowd or crush of scholars and opinions, and learned opinions and unlearned opinions about how the particular passage is to be understood. . . . [I]s it not true that all this seems to be rather complicated! God's Word is the mirror—in reading it or hearing it, I am supposed to see myself in

7. *FSE*, 25 / *SKS* 13, 53; italics removed.
8. Ibid.

the mirror—but look, this business of the mirror is so confusing that I very likely never come to see myself reflected—at least not if I go at it this way. One could almost be tempted to assume that the full force of human craftiness has a hand in it (alas, how true, in relation to God and godliness and God-fearing trust we humans are so crafty that we do not mean it at all when we tell each other that we are perfectly willing to do God's will if we only could find out what it is). One could almost be tempted to assume that this is craftiness, that we really do not want to see ourselves in that mirror and therefore we have concocted all this that threatens to make the mirror impossible, all this that we then honor with the laudatory name of scholarly and profound and serious research and pondering.[9]

In this all-too-modern age, we have found myriad ways of avoiding the truth of Scripture while at the same time continuing to read Scripture, or at least continuing to imagine we are doing so. After all, our eyes continue to scan the page, our minds continue to process the content of the sentences of the text. But in fact we are deluding ourselves into believing that we are "reading" when we are not really "reading" at all—at least not according to Kierkegaard's definition of the act.

It is unfortunately the case that one can spend one's whole life as a biblical scholar, poring over ancient sources and employing all known philological resources, publishing books, articles, and chapters in spades, without ever once asking what all this might mean for one's own life. A remedy is needed, and Kierkegaard supplies his readers with a mantra as antidote:

> [I]n order to see yourself in the mirror when you read God's Word you must (so that you actually do come to see yourself in the mirror) remember to say to yourself incessantly: It is I to whom it is speaking; it is I about whom it is speaking.[10]

9. *FSE*, 25–26 / *SKS* 13, 53–54.
10. *FSE*, 35 / *SKS* 13, 62; italics removed.

For Scripture to really be considered as Scripture for the reader, she must see herself as addressed in every one of its passages. All Scripture is truth *for me*, wants to tell *me* something—me in particular, a single individual.

Yet if we broaden for a moment our consideration of Kierkegaard's philosophy of reading, thinking back to chapter 1, we can see that this emphasis of personal address is not unique to Scripture. Everything should be read as if it has existential implications for my own life. There are distinctions to be made, especially in regard to the authority a text exercises over me (such authority being either direct or indirect, with Scripture and sermons falling into the former, and nearly everything else falling into the latter). Nevertheless, everything, properly considered, contains an address to me. It tells me: you must change your life. Not just Scripture contains this imperative. It should accompany every act of reading; thus existential metamorphosis is a part of Kierkegaard's philosophy of reading in general, not just when the reader approaches Scripture, but any text. All words can be used to enjoy God more fully. Every sentence can further lure us into obedience to divine imperatives.

Thus far, we have focused on the thematics of personal address rather than the ostensible subject of this chapter, action. This delay is intentional, for if you don't see how a text is addressing *you*—you in particular—it is difficult to see how it could spur you to action. In fact, this is just one of the many Kierkegaardian prerequisites to action that include all the topics covered so far. If you do not have conceptual clarity, it is likely you will not act in the right way; your "acts" will not truly count as actions because they are not in harmony with God's will; and if not in harmony with the eternal one, the One who is the only able to preserve, then your "acts" are mere ephemera, destined to dissipate into the nothingness toward which they tend. Curious reading blocks the subjective appropriation necessary to reading-guided action; in this mode of reading, there is never an "I" to whom the text is speaking. And if one's single individuality is not engaged and put at stake in the reading of a text, then there is no "I" to whom the text could even possibly speak.

There are, then, several prerequisites to Kierkegaardian action. Be that as it may, Kierkegaard is willing to set aside any and all of these ideally conceived prerequisites the moment they become temptations to inaction. At a certain point, Kierkegaard admonishes his readers: don't read, act! Set down this book! And in order to develop such a counterweight to all the seemingly necessary readerly prerequisites to action, Kierkegaard gives us a second metaphor: that of the love letter.

(2) The metaphor of the love letter begins with a one-word command: "Imagine." "Imagine," Kierkegaard bids us, "a lover who has received a love letter from his beloved";[11] and we should not skip over this word *Imagine*, for in it is contained a mini-philosophy of reading.

The good reader—the kind of reader Kierkegaard calls upon here—has the ability to imagine. What is entailed in this act? The answer is right there, in the root of the word: "imagine" is related to "image." A capable reader should be able to fashion an image for herself. Reading *Moby-Dick*, she should be able to picture a boat, an endless sea, a mighty whale; reading *For Self-Examination*, she should be able to make an image in her mind's eye of a love note being placed into a lover's hands. Yet, since we are not just visual creatures, a full imagining should entail multiple senses: a reader should smell salt water during an ocean narrative and touch the stiff white paper employed by love's effusions. Even beyond that, humans are creatures of intentionality, and so when we are told to "Imagine a lover who has received a love letter from his beloved," we should picture not only a visual and sensorial scene. We should imagine what it is like to *be* this lover, to be within his mind—to be filled with expectation, to have thought of nothing else for hours on end than to receive these words from the hand of the one who is cherished, upon whom one's happiness depends (and thus there must also be some trepidation when the letter is first opened). You yourself can likely provide a thousand variants on these few words

11. *FSE*, 26 / *SKS* 13, 54.

YOU MUST CHANGE YOUR LIFE

with which I have set the scene; most readers can be quite good at this sort of imagining, *if* they give themselves the time to practice it.

So then, imagine: gather all this together and create the scene. And what are we supposed to imagine? The lover receives a letter from his beloved, a simple tale immediately complicated by the following condition: the letter is written in a foreign language. The lover then sets hastily to work; grabbing a dictionary he "looks up every word in order to obtain a translation," which he goes about as quickly as he can.[12] It turns out, as he decodes the letter phrase by phrase, "that this letter from the beloved contained not only an expression of affection as such letters ordinarily do, but that it contained a wish, something that the beloved wished her lover to do."[13] Now, as soon as the lover comprehends the command, he immediately goes and does the action. It is a difficult task, and "any third party would consider that there was good reason to think better of it."[14] It is a difficult task, but the lover goes off right away and sets to it, without question.

Only, as it turns out, this action was not what the beloved wanted the lover to do. He has made an error in translation. When the beloved then arrives in person, she clarifies that this difficult action was not in fact her wish. But—and here Kierkegaard asks the crucial questions—"do you believe that he regrets the mistake, do you believe that he pleases his beloved less?"[15]

The implied answer to both these questions is an emphatic "No." The lover demonstrated his dedication to the beloved in his willingness to act; the fact of misinterpretation does not make the truth of the lover's subjective devotion any less true.

It is important to recognize that Kierkegaard has used a rhetorical exaggeration here to make his point. Taken in an overly literal fashion, Kierkegaard would seem to be saying: it does not

12. *FSE*, 26 / *SKS* 13, 54.
13. Ibid., 27 / 55.
14. Ibid., 27–28 / 55.
15. *FSE*, 28 / *SKS* 13, 56.

matter if an action is based on a correct interpretation of a text, all that matters is the passion with which the action is undertaken.

When placed in context, you can see this is not what Kierkegaard is claiming. The moral of the story is given shortly after its telling:

> In other words, when you are reading God's Word, it is not the obscure passages that bind you but what you understand, and with that you are to comply at once. If you understood only one single passage in all of Holy Scripture, well, then you must do that first of all, but you do not first have to sit down and ponder the obscure passages. If you do not read God's Word in such a way that you consider that the least little bit you do understand instantly binds you to do accordingly, then you are not reading God's Word.[16]

Less exaggeration is present in this passage, and Kierkegaard's point is clearer: what we do understand, we must act upon. Instead of acting, however, we have a tendency to retreat into reflective activity, pondering texts we do not understand. This, then, is the moral of the story: it is not that understanding or knowledge of concepts is unimportant. It is that we must act on those concepts we have understood, which we often do not do. Kierkegaard's rhetorical exaggeration is meant to shake his readers out of their lethargic state.

There are other passages where Kierkegaard exaggerates to achieve similar effects. As already discussed, in his *Works of Love* Kierkegaard makes a distinction between *Elskov* (romantic love) and *Kjerlighed* (agape). Late in *Works of Love*, Kierkegaard uses a specific example to illustrate this distinction: romantic love pursues the beloved, who is beautiful, whereas agape loves the neighbor, who is ugly.[17] This is an exaggeration. Kierkegaard does not mean we should love only ugly people nor that every neighbor is inherently repulsive. Rather, he means that we should love the neighbor without regard to her appearance. Even if the neighbor

16. Ibid., 29 / 57.
17. *WL*, 373 / *SKS* 9, 366–67.

is ugly, this should have no effect on whether or not we offer our love to this neighbor. Loving the neighbor who is ugly is only an exaggerated way of making a more measured point.

That we should act based on an interpretation even if it is mistaken is also an exaggerated way of making a more measured point. The point is that even if we understand very little of what we read, that does not excuse us from acting on that little. Again, "If you do not read God's Word in such a way that you consider that the least little bit you do understand instantly binds you to do accordingly, then you are not reading God's Word."[18]

Kierkegaard's insistence on action following immediately upon understanding is explicitly related, by him, to a philosophy of what Scripture is *for*: "God's Word is given in order that you shall act according to it, not that you shall practice interpreting obscure passages."[19] Yet—although he accords a higher authority to Scripture, or a greater ability for it to speak binding truth to its readers—the learning of concepts which direct action is the purpose of all reading, not just the reading of Scripture; and the reader is bound to act according to truth wherever she finds it. Simply put, reflection divorced from action is reflection separated from its purpose, whether one is reading Scripture or any other conceivable text.

The lover's reception of his beloved's letter, and his immediate obedience of its supposed wishes, serves to illustrate the principle that a true reading of a text involves an active response. Let's take two more examples in order to further clarify what Kierkegaard means, one taken from Scripture and the other not.

(1) Luke 18:22 reads "Sell everything you have and give to the poor" (NIV). This is not a difficult passage to understand. Melania the Younger understood it. She gave up her vast land holdings throughout the Roman empire and lived as a penurious nun from that point forward.[20] St. Francis of Assisi understood it: he gave all his wealth away, and even gave away the clothes on his back,

18. *FSE*, 29 / *SKS* 13, 57.

19. Ibid.

20. See Clark, *The Life of Melania, the Younger*.

leaving him stark naked in the middle of a church.[21] Francis then lived the rest of his life as a beggar—he lived "the highest poverty" in imitation of Christ and in obedience to the Scriptures.[22]

In short, Luke 18:22 is easy to understand. Yet, we wish to make it difficult. We do this by adding all kinds of obscure considerations: is this command supposed to be universal, or is it only addressed to the rich young ruler? Are all the Greek words translated correctly, or are there other linguistic possibilities? And, this passage—is it in all the original manuscripts? Perhaps it is not authentic, or there are major textual variants.

In Kierkegaard's mind, we have used scholarship in order to elevate understanding as an activity in itself to the point that acting on understanding has been nullified. He puts this charge to us in a brilliant passage that replays many of the themes just mentioned:

> It is only all too easy to understand the requirement contained in God's Word ("Give all your goods to the poor." "If anyone strikes you on the right cheek, turn the left." "If anyone takes your coat, let him have your cloak also." "Rejoice always." "Count it sheer joy when you meet various temptations" etc.). It is all just as easy to understand as the remark "The weather is fine today," a remark that could become difficult to understand in only one way—if a literature came into existence in order to interpret it. The most limited poor creature cannot truthfully deny being able to understand the requirement—but it is tough for flesh and blood to will to understand it and to have to act accordingly. In my view, it is human for a person to shrink from letting the Word really gain power over him—if no one else will admit it, I admit that I do. It is human to pray to God to have patience if one cannot immediately do what one should but still promises to strive; it is human to pray to God to have mercy, that the requirement is too high for one—if no one else will admit it, I admit that I do. But nevertheless it is not human to give the matter a totally different turn: that I cunningly shove in, one layer after another,

---

21. From Bonaventure's *Life of St. Francis*. See *Bonaventure,* 193–94.

22. See Agamben, *The Highest Poverty.*

interpretation and scholarly research (much in the way a boy puts a napkin or more under his pants when he is going to get a licking), that I shove all this between the Word and myself and then give this interpreting and scholarliness the name of earnestness and zeal for the truth, and then allow this preoccupation to swell to such prolixity that I never come to receive the impression of God's Word, never come to look at myself in the mirror. It seems as if all this research and pondering and scrutinizing would draw God's Word very close to me; the truth is that this is the very way, this is the most cunning way, to remove God's Word as far as possible from me, infinitely further than it is from one who never saw God's Word, infinitely further than it is from one who became so anxious and afraid of God's Word that he cast it as far away as possible.[23]

Note Kierkegaard's careful distinction: it is not that scholarship is in itself bad, but human selfishness has taken hold of scholarship and put it to its own malign purposes. Human nature doesn't want to be told to give everything away. Therefore, we read again, and again, and again, until the text doesn't tell us that any longer, or we are uncertain what exactly the text is telling us. This is where Kierkegaard shows up, grabs us by the shoulders, pulls us out of our chairs, pushes us out of our libraries and offices, and yells: Don't read, act!

(2) Our second example comes in the form of Natasha Trethewey's extraordinary poem, "Repentance." It is written in dialogue with Vermeer's painting *A Maid Asleep* (1656, Metropolitan Museum of Art, New York City), and reads as follows:

To make it right   Vermeer painted   then painted over
this scene   a woman alone at a table   the cloth pushed back
rough folds at the edge   as if   someone   had risen
in haste   abandoning the chair   beside her   a wineglass
nearly empty   just   in her reach   Though she's been called
idle and drunken   a woman drowsing   you might see

23. *FSE*, 34–35 / *SKS* 13, 61–62.

in her gesture   melancholia   Eyelids drawn
she rests   her head   in her hand   Beyond her   a still life
white jug   bowl of fruit   a goblet overturned   Before this
a man stood   in the doorway   a dog lay   on the floor
Perhaps   to exchange   loyalty   for betrayal
Vermeer erased   the dog   and made   of the man
a mirror   framed   by the open door   *Pentimento*
the word   for a painter's change   of heart   revision
on canvas   means the same   as remorse   after sin
Were she to rise   a mirror   behind her   the woman
might see   herself   as I did   turning   to rise
from my table   then back as if   into   Vermeer's scene
It was after   the quarrel   after   you'd had   again
too much   to drink   after   the bottle   did not shatter   though
I'd brought it   down hard   on the table   and the dog
had crept   from the room   to hide   Later   I found
a trace   of what I'd done   bruise on the table   the size
of my thumb   Worrying it   I must have looked   as she does
eyes downcast   my head   on the heel   of my palm   In paint
a story can change   mistakes be   undone   Imagine
Still Life   with Father   and Daughter   a moment so
far back   there's still time   to take the glass   from your hand
or mine[24]

This poem wants us to do something specific. We can spend hours looking at each fragmented line of verse, teasing out the poem's difficult rhythms; we can go to the Met, observing with closeness and care the intricacies of the poem's interaction with the Master's painting; we can place Trethewey's work within a broader lineage of ekphrastic verse;[25] we can look up the history of *pentimento* and discover what other famous paintings might display its traces. We can do all this, but if we do not reconcile with that one person, whom we love but from whom we are estranged—if we do not

24. Trethewey, *Monument*, 165–6.
25. See Denham, *Poets on Paintings*.

repent our anger while we still have the chance, we have missed Trethewey's meaning and have not really read the poem, at least not according to Kierkegaard's definition of the activity.[26]

Many kinds of books—not just Scripture—can bid us to act. Kierkegaard's philosophy of reading, especially as laid out in *For Self-Examination*, wants to insistently drive home this point: If you understand something, but don't act on it, you might as well not be reading at all. Thus: give everything and repent before it's too late.[27] You must act; you must change your life.

---

26. I like to imagine that the protagonist of David Lynch's wholesome, moving tale *The Straight Story* had read Trethewey's poem just before he set out on his tractor.

27. See Dillard, *Give It All, Give It Now*.

Conclusion

KIERKEGAARD'S PHILOSOPHY OF READING is rich and multifaceted, and is especially to be commended for being both spiritually oriented and capaciously welcoming of a variety of different types of literature. It also usefully recognizes that reading should be a limited activity; that is, if reading is all you are doing and all you want to do, it is likely you have not grasped the true purpose of reading. I hope I have convinced you of the truth of this positive assessment of the virtues of Kierkegaard's philosophy of reading over the preceding pages.

However, it does not follow from these virtues that Kierkegaard's philosophy of reading is without flaws. In conclusion, I will point out the flaw I consider to be most serious in Kierkegaard's philosophy of reading, and I offer a kind of corrective *via* a selected passage from St. Gregory of Nazianzus (329–390 AD), known in the Eastern Orthodox tradition as simply "Gregory the Theologian." In this way, I hope to present you, the reader, with a more complete philosophy of reading than Kierkegaard alone is able to provide.

Kierkegaard was a polemicist, and he admitted as much. Take a look at the following journal entry, written underneath the title "My Writings Considered as a 'Corrective' to the Established":

> The designation "corrective" is a category of reflection just as: here-there, right-left.

The person who is to provide the "corrective" must study the weak sides of the established scrupulously and penetratingly and then one-sidedly present the opposite—with expert one-sidedness. Precisely in this consists the corrective, and in this also the resignation in the one who is going to do it. In a certain sense the corrective is expended on the established.

If this is done properly, then a presumably sharp head can come along and object that "the corrective" is one-sided and get the public to believe there is something in what he says. Ye gods! Nothing is easier for the one providing the corrective than to add the other side; but then, right there, it ceases to be the corrective and itself becomes established order. Therefore an objection of this nature comes from a person utterly lacking the resignation required to provide "the corrective" and without even the patience to comprehend this.[1]

Kierkegaard thus writes polemically, as a corrective. His goal in writing was not to encompass all truth in a comprehensive system, but instead to push his readers in a certain direction as a response to the vices he perceived to be characteristic of his age.

In issuing his corrective, Kierkegaard at times takes an intentionally one-sided stance. This method of exaggeration affects his philosophy of reading, particularly when it comes to the relation between reading and acting (as covered in chapter 5).

The context for Kierkegaard's writings on the strict relation between reading and action—with true reading always issuing in action, and the sooner the better (even if haste causes error)—was a trend he had noted amongst his contemporaries: namely, a tendency to emphasize and exalt contemplation and comprehensive knowledge as goods in themselves. In Kierkegaard's assessment of his age, the one who actually acts is portrayed by society as embodying a vulgar exaggeration born of vanity.[2] In Golden Age Denmark, you could study mystics like Meister Eckhart, as Bishop

---

1. *JP* 6467 / *Pap.* X 1 A 640 n.d., 1849.
2. See especially *PC*, 58–59 / *SKS* 12, 71.

Hans Lassen Martensen did.[3] But to actually separate yourself off from society and seek out your own mystical experience of God—that would be an exaggeration. It would be to misunderstand the game that was being played. These extreme examples were to be studied as curious objects of scholarship, as embodying vastly different patterns of living that were entertaining for the comfortable modern citizen to learn about, but never actually to be emulated. It would be a haughty and presumptuous project to actually act upon one's reading of Meister Eckhart, for such action would produce in the course of one's life a stark difference from the social patterns regnant in the period of Golden Age Denmark.

Precisely this attitude is what drew Kierkegaard's ire, and he formulates his close, even inextricable, relation between reading and acting in response to it. This is an understandable response on Kierkegaard's part, but it does obscure an important truth about reading, one that other Christian theologians saw more clearly. (Perhaps their time periods and societies were less possessed of the vice of inaction, thus requiring less of a polemical reaction to correct against such a vice.)

The truth is this: reading is itself an act that transforms. When one reads, one has the opportunity to become the kind of person who enjoys reading, and that is, in itself, a transformation. This may seem a banal and obvious truth. When one places this truth in a broader anthropological context, however, its wisdom becomes manifest.

Human beings are creatures that enjoy. They take delight and pleasure in things. This fundamental truth about us can never be stamped out. It is not as if we can, by immense ascetic effort, completely remove this drive for enjoyment from ourselves. Rather: we will always be taking pleasure in something. The question is: What? Will it be a pleasure which is akin to a life of love for God, or not?

In his *Oration* 38, Gregory of Nazianzus recognizes this truth about human beings and proposes a way forward. He does so by

---

3. See Martensen, *Between Hegel and Kierkegaard.*

making a distinction between the Hellenic and the Christian festival, as follows:

> [L]et us leave these things to the Greeks and to Greek pomps and festivals. They name as gods those who enjoy the steam rising from the fat of sacrificed animals and correspondingly serve the divine with their stomachs, and they become evil fashioners and initiators and initiates of evil demons. But if we, for whom the Word is an object of worship, must somehow have luxury (τρυφᾶν, truphan),[4] let us have as our luxury the word and the divine law and narratives, especially those that form the basis of the present feast, that our indulgence may be akin and not foreign to the one who has called us.
>
> Would you like me—for I am your host today—to set before you, my good guests, a discourse as abundant and lavish as possible, that you may know how a stranger can feed the local inhabitants, and a rustic the city dwellers and one without pleasures the indulgent, and one poor and homeless those brilliant in wealth? I will begin from this point; and purify for me your mind and hearing and thoughts, you who enjoy luxuries of this kind, since the discourse is about God and divine things, that you may depart having truly received the luxuries that are not empty.[5]

Like Kierkegaard's distinction between *Elskov* and *Kjerlighed*, Gregory of Nazianzus wants us to achieve conceptual clarity by seeing the difference between Greek and Christian festivals. Notice, however, what that difference is predicated on. It is not the case that the Greek festival is dedicated to pleasure while the Christian festival is not. Rather, both festivals are completely devoted to pleasure (that is what makes them festivals). It is the case that the Greek festival is dedicated to some kinds of pleasure while

---

4. Harrison translates τρυφᾶν as "luxury" (*Festal Orations*, 64); Daley, *Gregory of Nazianzus*, 119, does the same. However, Paul Gallay translates τρυφᾶν as "*plaisirs*," or pleasure (*Sources Chrétiennes* 358, 113), a translation which also has much to commend it.

5. Gregory of Nazianzus, *Or*. 38.6 (*Sources Chrétiennes* 358, 112); *Festal Orations*, 64.

the Christian festival is devoted to others. According to Gregory of Nazianzus, Christians should give free rein to their desire for words. They should celebrate, indulge, and luxuriate in both written and spoken texts. This moment of contemplation, of sheer enjoyment, of delight at the interplay between rhetoric and reason, is a licit occupation for Christians, according to Gregory.

The Christian can thus be identified not only by what pleasures she rejects, but even more so by what she chooses to enjoy. This insight about the identity of the Christian points to the anthropology spoken of earlier, which is implicitly present in the text: namely, that human beings are animals who enjoy, who take delight and indulge pleasures. Becoming a Christian does not change this aspect of ourselves. Instead, it redirects it.

There are many objects of enjoyment that suffuse creation. Being a Christian means choosing some and rejecting others. After encountering Gregory of Nazianzus, one of those choices is clear. Being a Christian means choosing the pleasure of words. This is why becoming a devoted reader is *already* a change or transformation in the life of a human person. Works of love don't happen only after reading is finished. Sometimes reading itself is a work of love; it can be an activity that fundamentally changes who we are and draws us into new alignment with Christ the Word.

As stated, I believe Kierkegaard's press toward immediate action following upon the reading of words obscures this truth. However, it also provides an important check upon it. Truly, reading that does not eventually produce action is deficient, and Kierkegaard forcefully reminds us of this fact. You must change your life—even if, as a newly devoted reader, that change has already begun.

Bibliography

Adorno, Theodor W. *Kierkegaard: Construction of the Aesthetic*. Translated by Robert Hullot-Kentor. Minneapolis: University of Minnesota, 1989.
———. "On Kierkegaard's Doctrine of Love." *Zeitschrift für Socialforschung / Studies in Philosophy and Social Science*, 8, no. 3 (1939) 413–29.
Agamben, Giorgio. *The Highest Poverty: Monastic Rules and Form of Life*. Stanford, CA: Stanford University Press, 2013.
Alter, Robert. *The Prophets*. New York: W. W. Norton & Company, 2019.
Ameriks, Karl, ed. *The Cambridge Companion to German Idealism*. 2d ed. Cambridge: Cambridge University Press, 2017.
Augustine. *Confessions*. Translated by Henry Chadwick. Oxford: Oxford University Press, 1991.
———. *Teaching Christianity*. Translated by Edmund Hill, O.P. Hyde Park, NY: New City, 1996.
Aumann, Anthony. *Art and Selfhood: A Kierkegaardian Account*. Lanham, MD: Lexington, 2019.
Backhouse, Stephen. *Kierkegaard: A Single Life*. Grand Rapids: Zondervan, 2016.
Balthasar, Hans Urs von. *Heart of the World*. Translated by Erasmo Leiva. San Francisco: Ignatius, 1979.
Barnett, Christopher B. *Kierkegaard, Pietism and Holiness*. Farnham: Ashgate, 2011.
Barrett, Lee C. *Eros and Self-Emptying: The Intersections of Augustine and Kierkegaard*. Grand Rapids: Eerdmans, 2013.
Baudelaire, Charles. *The Painter of Modern Life and Other Essays*. Translated by Jonathan Mayne. London: Phaidon, 1995.
Berman, Patricia B. *In Another Light: Danish Painting in the Nineteenth Century*. New York: Vendome, 2007.
Bonaventure. *Bonaventure*. Classics of Western Spirituality. Translated by Ewert Cousins. Mahwah, NJ: Paulist, 1978.

Bokser, Ben Zion, and Baruch M. Bokser, eds. *The Talmud: Selected Writings.* Mahwah, NJ: Paulist, 1989.

Bonhoeffer, Dietrich. *Discipleship.* Translated by Barbara Green and Reinhard Krauss. Minneapolis: Fortress, 2001.

Carlisle, Clare. *Philosopher of the Heart: The Restless Life of Søren Kierkegaard.* London: Penguin, 2019.

Christensen, Villads. *Peripatetikeren Søren Kierkegaard.* Copenhagen: Graabrodre Torv, 1965.

Clark, Elizabeth A. *The Life of Melania, the Younger: Introduction, Translation, and Commentary.* Lewiston, NY: Edwin Mellen, 1984.

Daley, Brian E., S.J. *Gregory of Nazianzus.* London: Routledge, 2006.

Davenport, John J. "The Integration of Neighbor-Love and Special Loves in Kierkegaard and Von Hildebrand." In *Kierkegaard's God and the Good Life,* edited by Stephen Minister, J. Aaron Simmons, and Michael Strawser, 46–77. Bloomington, IN: Indiana University Press, 2017.

Deleuze, Gilles. *Nietzsche and Philosophy.* Translated by Hugh Tomlinson. New York: Columbia University Press, 1983.

Denham, Robert D. *Poets on Paintings: A Bibliography.* Jefferson, NC: McFarland & Co., 2010.

Dick, Kirby, and Amy Ziering Kofman, directors. *Derrida.* Jane Doe Films, 2002.

Dillard, Annie. *Give It All, Give It Now.* New York: Welcome, 2009.

Eagleton, Terry. *Literary Theory: An Introduction.* 3rd ed. Minneapolis: University of Minnesota Press, 2008.

Evans, C. Stephen. "Is Kierkegaard an Irrationalist? Reason, Paradox, and Faith." *Religious Studies,* vol. 25, no. 3 (September 1989) 347–62.

Fischer, Steven Roger. *A History of Reading.* London: Reaktion, 2019.

Garff, Joakim. *Kierkegaard's Muse: The Mystery of Regine Olsen.* Translated by Alastair Hannay. Princeton, NJ: Princeton University Press, 2017.

———. *Søren Aabye Kierkegaard: A Biography.* Translated by Bruce H. Kirmmse. Princeton, NJ: Princeton University Press, 2005.

Gregory of Nazianzus. *Festal Orations.* Translated by Nona Verna Harrison. Yonkers, NY: St. Vladimir's Seminary Press, 2008.

———. *Sources Chrétiennes* 358. Edited and translated by Paul Gallay. Paris: Les Éditions du Cerf, 1990.

Griffiths, Paul J. *Intellectual Appetite: A Theological Grammar.* Washington, DC: The Catholic University of America Press, 2009.

———. *Religious Reading: The Place of Reading in the Practice of Religion.* Oxford: Oxford University Press, 1999.

Hadot, Pierre. *Philosophy as a Way of Life: Spiritual Exercises from Socrates to Foucault.* Translated by Michael Chase. Oxford: Blackwell, 1995.

Hegel, Georg Wilhelm Friedrich. *Hegel's Preface to the* Phenomenology of Spirit. Translated with an introduction and running commentary by Yirmayahu Yovel. Princeton, NJ: Princeton University Press, 2005.

Holmer, Paul L. *On Kierkegaard and the Truth.* Eugene, OR: Cascade, 2012.

Hughes, Carl S. *Kierkegaard and the Staging of Desire: Rhetoric and Performance in a Theology of Eros.* New York: Fordham University Press, 2014.

Jacobs, Alan. *A Theology of Reading: The Hermeneutics of Love.* New York: Taylor & Francis, 2001.

Jennings, Willie James. *The Christian Imagination: Theology and the Origins of Race.* New Haven, CT: Yale University Press, 2010.

Kirmmse, Bruce H., ed. *Encounters with Kierkegaard: A Life as Seen by His Contemporaries.* Princeton, NJ: Princeton University Press, 1996.

Kirmmse, Bruce H. *Kierkegaard in Golden Age Denmark.* Bloomington, IN: Indiana University Press, 1990.

Levering, Matthew. *The Theology of Augustine: An Introductory Guide to His Most Important Works.* Grand Rapids: Baker Academic, 2013.

Løgstrup, Knud Ejler. *The Ethical Demand.* Translated by Theodore I. Jensen, Gary Puckering, and Eric Watkins. Notre Dame, IN: University of Notre Dame Press, 1997.

Luther, Martin. *Sermons.* Vol. 5. Translated by J. N. Lenker. Grand Rapids: Baker, 2000.

Lynch, David, director. *The Straight Story.* DVD. Walt Disney, 1999.

Manguel, Alberto. *A History of Reading.* New York: Penguin, 2014.

Marrs, Daniel J. "To Become Transfigured: Reconstructing Søren Kierkegaard's Christological Anthropology." PhD diss., Baylor University, 2015.

Martens, Paul, and Tom Millay, "Kierkegaard's Final Theodicy: God and the Gift of Suffering." *International Journal of Systematic Theology*, vol. 13, no. 2 (April 2011) 170–89.

Martensen, Hans Lassen. *Between Hegel and Kierkegaard: Hans Lassen Martensen's Philosophy of Religion.* Translated by Curtis L. Thompson and David J. Kangas. Oxford: Oxford University Press, 1997.

Millay, Thomas J. "Conceptual Clarity: Kierkegaard's Dialectical Method as a Response to the Religious Crisis of Golden Age Denmark." In *The Crisis of the Danish Golden Age and Its Modern Resonance*, edited by Jon Stewart and Nathaniel Kramer, 109–120. Copenhagen: Museum Tusculanum, 2020.

———. "Classical Greek Sculpture in *The Concept of Anxiety.*" In *Acta Kierkegaardiana VII: Kierkegaard and Classical Greek Thought,* edited by William McDonald and Andrew J. Burgess, 40–54. Toronto: Kierkegaard Circle, 2018.

———. "Concrete *and* Otherworldly: Reading Kierkegaard's *Works of Love* alongside Hegel's *Philosophy of Right.*" *Modern Theology,* vol. 34, no. 1 (January 2018) 23–41.

———. "You Must Change Your Life: Kierkegaard and Augustine on Reading." In *Kierkegaard and Augustine,* edited by Kim Paffenroth, John Doody, and Helene Tallon Russell, 169–78. Augustine in Conversation. Lanham, MD: Lexington, 2017.

Pattison, George. *Kierkegaard, Religion and the Nineteenth-Century Crisis of Culture.* Cambridge: Cambridge University Press, 2002.

BIBLIOGRAPHY

Pedersen, Mikkel Venbord, et al. *Danmark og kolonierne.* 5 vols. Copenhagen: Gads Forlag, 2017.

Peterson, Eugene. *Eat This Book: A Conversation in the Art of Spiritual Reading.* Grand Rapids: Eerdmans, 2006.

Podmore, Simon D. "The Lightening and the Earthquake: Kierkegaard on the *Anfechtung* of Luther." *The Heythrop Journal* XLVII (2006) 562–78.

Poole, Roger. "Towards a Theory of Responsible Reading: How to Read and Why." In *KSYB* 2002, 395–442.

Price, Leah. *What We Talk about When We Talk about Books: The History and Future of Reading.* New York: Basic, 2019.

Prior, Karen Swallow. *On Reading Well: Finding the Good Life through Great Books.* Grand Rapids: Brazos, 2018.

Schindler, D. C. *The Perfection of Freedom: Schiller, Schelling, and Hegel between the Ancients and the Moderns.* Eugene, OR: Cascade, 2012.

Sponheim, Paul R. *Existing before God: Søren Kierkegaard and the Human Venture.* Minneapolis: Fortress, 2017.

Stewart, Jon. *A History of Hegelianism in Golden Age Denmark, Tome I: The Heiberg Period: 1824-1836.* Copenhagen: C.A. Reitzel, 2007.

———. *A History of Hegelianism in Golden Age Denmark, Tome II: The Martensen Period: 1837-1842.* Copenhagen: C.A. Reitzel, 2007.

Stock, Brian. *Augustine the Reader.* Cambridge, MA: The Belknap Press of Harvard University Press, 1996.

Tietjen, Mark A. *Kierkegaard, Communication, and Virtue: Authorship as Edification.* Bloomington, IN: Indiana University Press, 2013.

Trethewey, Natasha. *Monument: Poems New and Selected.* Boston: Houghton Mifflin Harcourt, 2018.

Turchin, Sean Anthony. "Appropriation." In *KRSRR*, Volume 15, Tome I, 83–87.

Turnbull, Jamie. "Communication/Indirect Communication." In *KRSRR*, Volume 15, Tome II, 17–23.

Wilson, E. O. "Enemy Specification in the Alarm-Recruitment System of an Ant." *Science*, New Series, vol. 190, no. 4216 (November 21, 1975) 798–800.

———. *Naturalist.* Washington, DC: Island, 1994.

Wilson, E. O. and Bert Hölldobler. *The Ants.* Cambridge, MA: Harvard University Press, 1990.

Name and Subject Index

Scripture Index

www.ingramcontent.com/pod-product-compliance
Lightning Source LLC
Chambersburg PA
CBHW020211090426
42734CB00008B/1022